Praise for
The Novice Advantage

Dr. Eckert's new book is a must read for every novice—and the teacher educators who prepare them for the realities of the early years of teaching. While filled with practical advice for the new recruit, his book also serves as an antidote for the scripted recipes foisted upon too many classroom novices today. *The Novice Advantage* does not offer 63 steps to teaching effectiveness heaven but a blueprint for developing capacity to teach effectively over time and learning to lead the profession that students and our public schools deserve.

Barnett Berry
Founder and CEO,
Center for Teaching Quality

An insightful and refreshing reminder for aspiring teacher leaders and those continually developing their expertise. Dr. Eckert highlights the value of seeking those "first days" throughout our careers—that the joy and nervousness experienced in these transformational moments are critical to have again and again if we are to grow personally and professionally. Dr. Eckert highlights valuable resources and processes that all educators need for this journey.

Patrick Ledesma
Director of Research and Knowledge Management,
National Board for Professional Teaching Standards

Stories are a powerful way to learn. Eckert reminds us of this critical lesson more effectively than anyone in recent times. In his casting of continued development through the fresh eyes of the novice, he provides us with a special gift. You will leave *Novice* as a better teacher—and a wiser one as well.

Joseph Murphy
Frank W. Mayborn Chair of Education and
Associate Dean at Peabody College of
Education at Vanderbilt University

With humor and grace, Jon Eckert challenges every teacher to let go of practices that restrain them in favor of practices that allow them to grow. The journey of personal growth means recapturing the hopefulness of novice teachers. As he writes, Eckert bares his deep belief that all individuals have the capacity for continued growth, that even long-experienced veterans can get out of their ruts and tap into their deep wells of knowledge and abilities in the pursuit of improving school for all children.

Joan Richardson
Editor-in-chief,
Phi Delta Kappan

Jonathan Eckert explores and expounds a crucial tenet of effective teaching and instructional improvement: When we take risks, when we fail, when we reflect, and when we revise, we are constantly learning. And when we are constantly learning we are increasing the odds that we will be continuously successful. Eckert invites us into the often terrifying, disorienting, but exhilarating world of novice teachers to drive this point home. In a counter-intuitive but clear and convincing argument, Eckert tells us that we would all be better teachers if we were to be more like novices in this regard, always learning through risk, reflection, and revision, as if we too had little choice in the matter. This is an engaging, insightful, and instructive read. I strongly recommend it to prospective, novice, and experienced teachers and to those who help prepare and support them.

Mark A. Smylie
Professor Emeritus, College of Education,
University of Illinois at Chicago

If you're ready to laugh, cry, wince, sigh, and nod about classroom adventures (others' and your own), this book is for you. The stories will resonate with any teacher who has had a "cringeworthy" classroom moment or two. As an experienced educator, I began reading Jon's insightful analysis expecting to come away with a renewed reminder of the "novice" world; instead, I was schooled by a great teacher. We are ALL novices and should strive to stay in that space. It's where lifelong learners hang out. Because we all begin something new each day, this book is not only for novice teachers—it's for all teachers who want to get better.

Ann Byrd
COO and Partner,
Center for Teaching Quality

Jon Eckert shifts the conversation—and hopefully our mindsets—regarding growth and learning as educators, no matter where we are in our career. In his book *The Novice Advantage*, Eckert highlights the importance of thinking of ourselves as novices who are constantly growing instead of experts complacent with our practice. This book pushes our thinking on expertise as educators and is great fodder for book groups, professional learning communities, or any collaborative professional conversation. A must-read!

Megan Allen
Director, Master of Arts in Teacher Leadership,
Mount Holyoke College

I found myself laughing and taking notes throughout the book. Jon's ability to weave humor with proven, field-tested techniques will empower both new educators and veterans alike.

Mawi Asgedom
Founder of Mawi Learning and author of
Of Beetles and Angels: One Boy's Journey from a
Refugee Camp to Harvard

So often we aspire to expertise with the false notion that experts are infallible. In *The Novice Advantage*, Jon Eckert paints a more realistic picture—that it's actually failures and rigorous reflective practice that breeds expertise. With deep case studies, practical strategies based in research, and amusing anecdotes, this book is a particularly useful addition to the tool belt of any professional, at any stage of their career. My recent shift from the classroom to teacher leader, then to nonprofit leadership have forced me to rely on my Novice Advantage—I only wish the book was published while I was still in the classroom.

Nick Greer
Managing Director of Programs, Thread, and
Former Director of Science in Baltimore City Public Schools

Eckert's book belongs in the hands of aspiring teachers and master teachers alike. He brings a writer's touch and a teacher's insight into what it means for educators to be lifelong learners in the context of their career.

Brad Jupp
Senior Program Advisor on Teacher Initiatives,
U.S. Department of Education

If you see teaching as a step on a career ladder, don't read this book. But if you see teaching as a lifelong craft, worthy of a lifetime's dedication, this book is written for you. Our education system has plenty of resources to help first-year teachers become competent. *The Novice Advantage* is written for those of us who want to move beyond competence to excellence. Jon Eckert writes "We need teachers who innovate, risk, create, reflect, and grow." This book is written for that kind of teacher.

Justin Minkel
Second-Grade Teacher and 2007 Arkansas Teacher of the Year,
Jones Elementary, Springdale, AR

Jon Eckert has given the profession a gift we desperately need. Real help and real inspiration for real novice teachers (and those of us with a few more years under the bridge). It comes at a critical juncture, when the median years of service among teachers in the U.S. is one year. Unlike too many books for new teachers, this is not filled with quick tips or rote formulas, but rather with thoughtful, useful advice anchored in the reality of teaching in America today. Most of all, it is genuine encouragement, reminding us that teaching is a calling that requires systematic preparation, demands significant sacrifice, but yields eternal rewards.

Renee Moore
@TeachMoore, NBCT, blogger, author,
Center for Teaching Quality

The epitome of an "expert novice" himself, Eckert offers teachers at all stages of the profession clear, precise, and inspiring strategies for reaching students. And by recognizing the contributions educators make both inside and outside the classroom to shape great teaching, he elevates the teacher voice to its rightful position at the forefront of any discussion about the daily work of our schools.

Jocelyn Pickford
Designer of the Teaching Ambassador Fellowship at the
U.S. Department of Education

The Novice Advantage empowers the hopefulness of education. It provides practical ways for beginning and veteran teachers to maintain their enthusiasm and wonder of teaching.

This book covers, in a very clear, useful, and readable fashion, all the relevant and effective strategies of a successful teacher. This could very well be the only book an aspiring or veteran teacher would need to fill their instructional toolbox. The "Key Takeaways and Fearless Practices" sections at the end of each chapter provide a quick resource of reminders to strategies that will bolster continued reflection and improvements. It is a must-read for all educators.

A powerful concept that is seldom considered is what Dr. Eckert refers to as "getting better at getting better through honest reflection and transparent practice." It's the notion focusing on improvement rather than what was wrong and looking in the windshield instead of the rearview mirror.

Robert A. Rammer
Assistant Superintendent,
Wheaton Warrenville Community Unit School District #200

This book is an authentic, honest, and humorous depiction of teaching. Dr. Eckert captures the heart of veteran teachers as well as novice teachers and tells the story of a profession that is unlike any other. This book ignites the

passion of teaching and encourages all of us to try new things and "live on the edge"!

Tammie Schrader
Regional Science Coordinator at Educational Service District 101,
Spokane, Washington

The Novice Advantage is an inspiring call to educators to make continuous learning and improvement central to their own teaching, as well as highlighting how important it is for teachers to participate in broader efforts to transform school and district structures to support continuous growth for all teachers and students.

Kristan Van Hook
Senior Vice President for Policy,
National Institute for Excellence in Teaching

For my students and Carolyn, Ben, Sarah, and Grace—
You give me many opportunities to learn and grace to grow.

The Novice Advantage
Fearless Practice for Every Teacher

Jonathan Eckert

CORWIN
A SAGE Publishing Company

FOR INFORMATION:

Corwin

A SAGE Company

2455 Teller Road

Thousand Oaks, California 91320

(800) 233-9936

www.corwin.com

SAGE Publications Ltd.

1 Oliver's Yard

55 City Road

London EC1Y 1SP

United Kingdom

SAGE Publications India Pvt. Ltd.

B 1/I 1 Mohan Cooperative Industrial Area

Mathura Road, New Delhi 110 044

India

SAGE Publications Asia-Pacific Pte. Ltd.

3 Church Street

#10-04 Samsung Hub

Singapore 049483

Acquisitions Editors: Erin Null and
                        Ariel Bartlett

Associate Editor: Desirée A. Bartlett

Editorial Assistant: Andrew Olson

Production Editor: Amy Schroller

Copy Editor: Tammy Giesmann

Typesetter: C&M Digitals (P) Ltd.

Proofreader: Eleni-Maria Georgiou

Indexer: Judy Hunt

Cover Designer: Gail Buschman

Marketing Manager: Jill Margulies

Printed in the United States of America

Library of Congress Cataloging-in-Publication Data

Names: Eckert, Jonathan, author.

Title: The novice advantage : fearless practice for every teacher / Jonathan Eckert.

Description: Thousand Oaks, California : Corwin, a SAGE company, 2016. | Includes bibliographical references and index.

Identifiers: LCCN 2015045196 | ISBN 9781506328744 (pbk. : alk. paper)

Subjects: LCSH: First year teachers. | Teachers—In-service training. | Teaching—Psychological aspects. | Motivation in education.

Classification: LCC LB2844.1.N4 E35 2016 | DDC 370.71/1—dc23 LC record available at http://lccn.loc.gov/2015045196

This book is printed on acid-free paper.

SFI Certified Sourcing
www.sfiprogram.org
SFI-00453

16 17 18 19 20 10 9 8 7 6 5 4 3 2 1

Contents

Preface

There is something about big yellow buses, adolescents, bumpy roads, and junk food that induce nausea. I was a new teacher, and my class was on one of those buses traveling down the Eisenhower Expressway to the Field Museum in Chicago.

> I noticed a male student turning an odd shade of green—you know the color.
>
> The driver could not stop.
>
> I could not get back to him with the trashcan.
>
> His window was open.
>
> You know where this is going.
>
> Inexplicably, I yelled, "Put your head out the window!"
>
> Dutifully, he complied.

As a science teacher, I feel compelled to tell you that when traveling at 52 miles per hour down an expressway, any liquid that exits a window will come back in the next four windows and cover anyone unlucky enough to be sitting nearby. Suddenly, I had four more students turning that same shade of green and a significant cleanup job.

Lesson: Don't tell a student to spray his vomit on four other students.

This year marks the eighteenth anniversary of this incident, and I am reminded of why I am writing this book. The incident could happen to almost anyone and did not make me a dramatically better teacher, but mistakes like this beg the question: How do we get better as teachers—not just individually, but as a profession?

THE NOVICE ADVANTAGE

One way we get better is through first days. In an ever-changing education landscape, we have to change, which means we have many first days over the course of our careers. We get to begin again every fall. Below are some of my first days and the thoughts and feelings I associate with them:

- First day as a student teacher: *Awkward excitement*—I am a guest in someone else's classroom, but I am so excited that I am finally teaching.

- First day of teaching: *Pure joy tempered by fear*—I have real students! This is our classroom. I can't believe parents are going to trust me with their children.

- First day of teaching middle school students: *???*—What am I doing in a science lab with middle schoolers? Did I make a mistake? Didn't I hate middle school as a student? I can make middle school better for these students. I get to teach science all day!

- First day as a doctoral student at Vanderbilt University: *Overwhelmed enthusiasm* —Am I really a student again? My fellow doctoral students are way smarter than I am. Will I survive the next three years of teaching, coaching, and Vanderbilt? I am excited.

- First day at the U.S. Department of Education: *Restrained optimism*—Teachers are actually going to be able to influence federal education policy. Is this really true?

- First day as a college professor: *Curiosity*—Can I help prepare better teachers, conduct research, influence policy, and continue to grow as a teacher?

- First day back in a fifth grade classroom: *Playful innovation*—As a professor, I have time go to local public schools and teach real kids. My college students give me feedback. Am I still growing as an effective teacher?

I have grown through all of these first days. Whether we like it or not, our work as teachers continues to change. We get new students, new standards, new curriculum, new technology, or new demands. We can either be overwhelmed or embrace the possibilities that come from new opportunities. When we choose to embrace them, they become an advantage when we take on the "novice mindset."

The novice *mindset* is the belief that we grow continuously through fearless, deliberate practice. When we are new, we seek input, adapt, change, and are constantly learning. There is an exciting rawness to that learning, which can make teaching utterly fascinating, and thus becomes advantageous. The novice *advantage* is therefore the benefit that comes from fully embracing the notion that we can get better each year, each semester, each class period, and each field trip. When we embrace this mindset, we become open to the bold practice—free of fear—needed to meet the diverse needs of today's classrooms.

Getting better requires deliberate practice (Dweck, 2006; Ericsson, Krampe, & Tesch-Romer, 1993; Hattie & Yates, 2014; National Research Council, 2000; Willingham, 2009). We know deliberate practice is necessary for students—skills

> The novice mindset is the belief that we grow continuously through fearless, deliberate practice.

need to be developed with guidance, specific goals, feedback, assessment, and reflection (Hattie & Yates, 2014). We provide this for students every day. However, this kind of practice is rare for teachers due to lack of opportunity and fear in this current educational system. *Teach Like a Novice* is designed to help change that reality for every teacher.

WHO NEEDS THIS?

Most of us are not superhero teachers. Maybe, we dreamed we would be when we watched Robin Williams stand on his desk and tell his students to rip pages out of textbooks in *Dead Poet's Society*. Maybe Edward James Olmos inspired us to push calculus students to *Stand and Deliver*. We wanted to be Michelle Pfeiffer inspiring students to become *Dangerous Minds*, or Hilary Swank developing *Freedom Writers*, or Viola Davis who *Won't Back Down*, or Richard Dreyfuss as he conducts *Mr. Holland's Opus*, or maybe we just want to be the *Superman* that students are *Waiting for*.

I certainly am not a superhero teacher. The first time I saw myself teach on videotape I knew that no one would be making a movie about my teaching. My students have ripped pages out of their textbooks in my classes, but not for principled reasons. Students have done things to their desks but not because I wanted them to. Although some of the movies listed above are based on true stories, these depictions have been glorified and sensationalized. They do not capture the genuine realities of teaching.

The actors in these movies are not real teachers.

This book is for real teachers. Preservice, beginning, experienced, inspired, naïve, savvy, committed, and tired teachers. Any teachers who want to get better. *The Novice Advantage* is about a mindset and process that can be applied to practices over the entirety of a teaching career. Real teachers need to be fearlessly vulnerable and honest in their reflection on their teaching as evidenced by student learning. Expert teachers do this well. In order to become experts—not just experienced—we need the novice mindset.

The novice mindset is accompanied by a process composed of the "Four Rs:" reflect, risk, revise or reject. Coupled with the mindset, this process is necessary for deliberate practice to achieve expertise or status as an "expert novice." Great teachers engage in this process regardless of how many years they have been teaching. There are richer examples of practice throughout the book, but briefly, here are the Four Rs:

1. Reflect: Student is turning green on bus. From previous experience, I know something bad is about to happen.

2. Risk: Tell student to stick head out the window to avoid mess on the bus (a particularly bad idea when hands and arms are not even allowed outside the window).

3. and 4. Reflect then Revise or Reject: Four students ended up covered in vomit. Reject any suggestion of having student use a window on a fast moving bus as a means of emptying his stomach.

A WAY FORWARD

The Novice Advantage is for every teacher who wants to get better. If you can only read this for three minutes at a time before falling into a coma each night, you should be able to get something you can use the next day. I understand and appreciate your exhaustion. I have been there with my face mashed against a book, with saliva pooling on a page as I lay unconsciously hoping some knowledge will be gained through osmosis.

A WAY BACK

Some of us have not been novices for a long time and might be a bit put off by the title of this book. We remember back to when we were novices, and we cringe. But, we also remember the energy, passion, and desire for learning we had. Remember how we were desperately learning, sometimes minutes before class began, and how our students, our school community, and the craft of teaching fascinated us? Remember the courage it took to stand in front of our students that first time or make it through that first night of parent-teacher conferences? Remember what it was like to not know all of the reasons why something won't work? This book offers a way back to the great aspects of the novice mindset while building on the teaching expertise we now have.

USE THIS BOOK TO MAKE YOUR WORK EASIER

This book will make your work easier. I despise books and professional development that make me feel like I just need to work harder and longer when I am already stretched thinner than seems healthy. Throughout the book, you'll find features that will make your work easier and stretch your thinking further.

First, you'll find many ideas for practices and strategies you can implement in your classroom immediately. You don't have to overhaul your practice, but some innovative thinking and small adjustments, borne out of your novice mindset, can go a long way.

Second, throughout the chapters, I include stories of amazing and cringe-worthy practice, the latter coming largely at my expense that will make you feel better about the work you do (you probably feel better already because you have never told a student to stick his head out the window of a moving bus to vomit). You will be inspired by the work you do with your colleagues and with your students but not in a way that feels overwhelming.

Third, *The Novice Advantage* has boxes throughout each chapter that ask for "fearless reflection." These boxes ask you to evaluate districts, schools, and yourself so that you can honestly approach improvement—you have to be fearless to do this. At the end of each chapter are discussion questions, open-ended case studies, and 3-2-1 action steps that allow you to apply what you are learning. Throughout the book are graphics, case studies, and side-bars that summarize key research that you can easily apply to your work. Ideally, we are journeying through our teaching careers with trusted colleagues. That is the ideal way to engage this book—in a class, professional learning community, virtual community, or book group. Superhero teachers, at least the ones in the movies, always appear to be fighting alone against the system and often their colleagues, too. This book is designed for us to get better together to improve the system for everyone—maybe we will all become superhero teachers. Given how valuable our work is, I hope we do become superhero teachers, but I hope we will be more of a team than individuals acting alone—think more Avengers and fewer Spidermen.

HOW THIS BOOK IS ORGANIZED

The book is divided into three parts:

Part I. Novice Mindset and Process—Chapters 1–3

Part II. Practices—Chapters 4–7

Part III. Expert Novices—Chapter 8

Part I will introduce the novice mindset and lead you through the 4R process. In Chapter 1, you will find cringeworthy moments from novice teaching and see how these can lead to continuous learning in a rapidly changing field. Chapter 2 asks you to embrace the novice mindset for yourself and your students. Chapter 3 describes the process that will facilitate disciplined risk taking that informs and is informed by practice.

Part II encourages you to apply the novice mindset and 4Rs to essential practices of effective teaching. In Chapter 4, you will explore ways to expand the walls of your classroom to increase the space for thinking, hard work, and risk taking. Chapter 5 addresses the challenges of motivating students who may not be particularly interested in your class, are not intrinsically motivated, or do not believe they can succeed in school. Chapter 6 will explore ways of expecting more of your students and how to operationalize those expectations. In Chapter 7, you will find strategies for developing relationships with students and other essential partners that make education possible.

Part III will help you become a fearless expert novice at whatever point you may be in your career. With the novice mindset and the 4Rs applied to good practice, teaching is rewarding and renewing. With this mindset and tools, you will fearlessly lead your students and our profession.

The Novice Advantage is a testament to the amazing teachers I know who hope for a better profession for teachers and better outcomes for our students. You might not like all of the ideas in the book, but that is part of the mindset and process—in fact, disagreeing means that you are engaging with the ideas. Think of this as a professional conversation between real teachers about real teaching, real students, and real learning. Maybe they won't make movies about us, but that's okay because we really just want to get better for our students.

Acknowledgments

This book is the product of what I have learned from so many amazing teachers. There is no way I could possibly acknowledge everyone who has impacted this project. My colleagues at Emerson School, Poplar Grove School, Vanderbilt University, the U.S. Department of Education, and Wheaton College have played a significant part in shaping this book. Many of them are the exemplary teachers highlighted on these pages.

My students are the reason I teach and many of them provided excellent suggestions—particularly Elissa McAlvey, Whitney Hall, and my Wheaton College research team. McKenna Fitzharris volunteered hours of her summer to read and revise every chapter. My department colleagues, particularly Patti McDonnell, Mark Jonas, Sara Vroom, and Sally Morrison were always willing to brainstorm ideas with me. My department chairs, Jill Lederhouse and Paul Egeland helped me make space to write this book. My senior seminar class, along with Betsy Leong's class, provided outstanding feedback throughout their student teaching semesters. Betsy trusted me enough to assign the book draft as required reading.

Barnett Berry and Ann Byrd of the Center for Teaching Quality have offered invaluable advice and support over the last five years and have made this book significantly better. The Teaching Ambassador Fellows were exemplary models of teaching and provided helpful suggestions. Jasmine Ulmer and Tammie Schrader provided particularly helpful clarity. Joan Dabrowski and Mark Smylie, both excellent writers, made me a more thoughtful writer and provided very useful ideas and books to read. Erik Ellefsen and I have been talking about the topics in this book for over a decade, and he read many drafts. He is a great educator and better friend.

Joan Richardson, editor-in-chief at *Phi Delta Kappan*, published the article that was the impetus for this book and has always provided great encouragement. I am tremendously grateful to Corwin and Arnis Burvikovs for reaching out to me about writing this book after reading the piece in *Kappan*. The Corwin team has been extremely helpful—Andrew Olson took care of the details, Ariel Price offered helpful direction, and Erin Null, my thoughtful editor, guided my writing process with insightful feedback.

Finally, my family deserves tremendous credit for indulging my steady stream of random thoughts and book revisions. There is nothing like getting suggestions for how to improve teaching from a seventh, fourth, and second grader—thanks Ben, Sarah, and Grace. I am so grateful to my wife Carolyn who read *many* iterations of this book and tried not to allow her eyes to glaze over when I talked about teaching for hours. She makes many sacrifices and is remarkably patient with me—she is my best friend.

PUBLISHER'S ACKNOWLEDGMENTS

Corwin gratefully acknowledges the contributions of the following reviewers:

Gustava Cooper-Baker
Adjunct Professor
University of Central Missouri
Kansas City, MO

Katie Morrow
Instructional Technology Facilitator
Educational Service Unit #8
Neligh, NE

Randy Wormald
Teacher
Kearsarge Regional School District
North Sutton, NH

Marianne R. Young
Principal
Monument Mountain Regional
    High School
Great Barrington, MA

Rosemarie Young
Field Placement Coordinator
Bellarmine University
Louisville, KY

About the Author

Jonathan Eckert was a public school teacher outside of Chicago and Nashville for twelve years. He earned his doctorate in education at Vanderbilt University and served as a U.S. Department of Education Teaching Ambassador Fellow in both the Bush and Obama administrations. Currently, he is an associate professor of education at Wheaton College where he prepares teachers and returns regularly to teach in the district where his career began. In addition to leading professional development across the country, he has published numerous peer-reviewed and practitioner articles on teaching and education policy.

PART I
Mindset and Processes

CHAPTER 1

Cringeworthy Moments

Why Would I Want to Be a Novice?

"An expert is a man who has made all of the mistakes that can be made in a very narrow field."

—Niels Bohr
Nobel Prize–winning physicist

The year was 1995. Picture a room filled with thirty-two fourth-grade students arranged in groups of three or four. I am the earnest student teacher at the front of the room teaching a lesson that should have lasted ten to fifteen minutes. I am enthusiastically teaching for nearly forty-five minutes. Four students are remarkably engaged, but I really have no idea what the other twenty-eight students are doing as I am passionately inspiring these four students. My cooperating teacher sits in the back of the room, cringing behind the camera, recording this antithetical example of pedagogical content knowledge (Shulman, 1986). Mercifully for twenty-eight students, my lesson finally ends. My cooperating teacher says very little to me. However, there is a devious twinkle in his eye when he requests that I sit down and watch the video with him.

I wonder what sadistic enjoyment he hopes to take from this, but I agree. I did not really have a choice. After school, we sit down and put the VHS tape in the VCR. I don't know why I am sweating, but this is a miserable experience. However, it is not that bad . . . for the first five minutes. Then, I actually get bored watching myself. At about the twenty-eight minute mark, without me noticing, the camera slowly pans to the left side of the room, which should have been in my peripheral vision. A male student has his knees on his chair and is absentmindedly humping his desk. This "activity" continues for nearly five minutes. The camera is actually shaking because my cooperating teacher was laughing so hard. Neither the student nor the highly amused cooperating teacher was a big enough cue to make me aware while teaching. I became aware of this student's extremely off-task behavior when watching this video of him and twenty-seven other students disengaging from the lesson.

I know I was not the only new teacher to struggle. I get the opportunity to watch beginning teachers struggle all the time as a professor and student teaching supervisor. I sit in the back of student teachers' classrooms watching disaster after disaster unfold before me. Here are a few vignettes from my supervision notes:

- Student has been loudly sharpening his pencil for three minutes—and only stopped because he ran out of pencil.

- Teacher just gave student her third warning before having her move her stoplight to yellow, which itself is . . . A WARNING!

- Two students are physically fighting in their chairs at the back of the classroom. *How is it possible to fight entirely below desk level while seated?*

You may be checking the cover to this book and wondering why anyone would suggest that there is a novice advantage. You certainly have a vision of struggling teachers from these examples.

Aren't we supposed to be striving to be experts instead? Certainly, there is a great divide between experts and novices. We also know that experience does not equal expertise (Hattie & Yates, 2014). To gain expertise, we need deliberate practice—practice that includes guidance, goals, objective assessment, feedback, and reflection (Ericsson, Krampe, & Tesch-Romer, 1993; Hattie & Yates, 2014). As painful as watching ourselves teach on video can be, if coupled with guidance, goals, assessment, feedback, and reflection, this can be a powerful tool for growth (Knight, 2014).

Experts notice features and patterns, organize knowledge in ways that demonstrate deep understanding, can flexibly retrieve knowledge, can "chunk" information, and have many hours of deliberate practice (Berliner, 2004; Hattie & Yates, 2014; National Research Council, 2000). In his best selling book, *Outliers,* Malcolm Gladwell (2008) popularized the notion that experts in fact need ten thousand hours of deliberate practice (Ericsson et al., 1993) in a particular area to become experts. That is over eight years of teaching, *if* all of that teaching is deliberate practice.[1] Researchers have illustrated the benefits of experience for student learning (Ladd & Sorensen, 2014; Papay & Kraft, in press). However, experienced teachers are not necessarily expert teachers (Hargreaves & Fullan, 2012).

We have no idea what classrooms will look like ten years from now. Embracing change, or standing firm on principled practice will require reflection, risk taking (sometimes not changing is a risk), and a novice mindset. Traditional teacher preparation programs, alternative route providers, teacher residencies, and district mentoring and induction programs must

---

[1] That is 8.5 years if a teacher has 6.5 hours of student contact time per day for 180 days per year. Teaching obviously entails far more than student contact time, but you get the idea—expertise takes a while to develop.

Expert teachers often develop

- automaticity and routinization for the repetitive operations that are needed to accomplish their goals;

- sensitivity to the task demands and social situation when solving pedagogical problems;

- flexibility in their teaching;

- ability to represent problems in qualitatively different ways than do novices;

- fast and accurate pattern recognition;

- problem-solving ability that may be slower than novices, but brings a richer and more personal source of information to bear on the problem they are trying to solve . . .

Expertise is specific to a domain, and to particular contexts in domains, and is developed over hundreds and thousands of hours (2004, p.13).

help novices capitalize on these strengths. This is essential for our system as the modal years (most frequently reported—think mean, median, and *mode*) of experience for U.S. teachers is one. This means that the most common teacher by experience is a first-year teacher (Ingersoll, Merrill, & Stuckey, 2014).

In order to become experts we must first be novices, as Niels Bohr's quote at the beginning of this chapter recommends. He was a Nobel Prize winning Danish physicist, in addition to being a 1908 Olympian in soccer, who gave the world the Bohr model of the atom and the foundation to understand much of what we know about quantum physics. A man as gifted as Bohr attributes his success to making mistakes. He reflected on them and learned from them. James Joyce, renowned author, took this even further. He wrote in *Ulysses*, "A man of genius makes no mistakes. His errors are volitional and are the portals of discovery." When we stop reflecting, risking, and revising our attempts, we stop learning.

THE NOVICE ADVANTAGE

This is the distinct advantage of maintaining a novice mindset. People that are successful in any profession are constantly learning—risking, reflecting, and revising. In today's changing economic, cultural, and educational conditions, learning and application of that learning may be more valuable than knowledge. In fact, as prolific writer Parker Palmer points out, there is tremendous value in being a novice. "To get unstuck, I must let go of my 'career' as an established writer and begin again as a novice. In truth I am a novice in every new moment of the day, each of which presents possibilities unknown and untried" (Palmer, 2015).

In today's changing economic, cultural, and educational conditions, learning and application of that learning may be more valuable than knowledge.

While writing for a business audience, Liz Wiseman (2014) identifies the curious and flexible mindset of rookies. Her team's research indicates that rookies have significantly higher levels of self-awareness, are more likely to seek out expertise, tend to deliver more timely solutions, and are more attuned to politics than veterans in business. She describes four mindsets that provide a rookie advantage. Effective rookies are Backpackers, Hunter-Gatherers, Firewalkers, and Pioneers.

Novices as Backpackers vs. Veterans as Caretakers: Rookies in business are open to new possibilities, unencumbered, and do not rely on habits and practices of the past. Veterans can become Caretakers. Having demonstrated previous success, they seek to protect their gains and maintain the status quo.

Novices as Hunter-Gathers vs. Veterans as Local Guides: Rookies lack knowledge so they seek out experts and return with ideas and resources. Veterans can become Local Guides who stick to what they know and offer advice.

Novices as Firewalkers vs. Veterans as Marathoners: Rookies take small, calculated steps but move quickly and seek feedback. Veterans can become Marathoners when they pace themselves and plod along assuming they are still doing good work.

Novices as Pioneers vs. Veterans as Settlers: Rookies keep things simple and focus on meeting basic needs while improvising and pushing boundaries. Veterans can become settlers when they are protecting territory and remaining in their comfort zones.

(from Wiseman, 2014)

Echoing what I hear from beginning, veteran, and accomplished teachers across this country, we need teachers who innovate, risk, create, reflect, and grow. "Teaching is a natural, human act that occurs between humans who express a desire to connect with each other and join their knowledge" (Rodriguez & Fitzpatrick, 2014, p. 19). The classroom has to be an exciting place to grow. For twenty years (including a one-year-long interlude at the U.S. Department of Education), that has been what the classroom has been for me. I constantly go back to my first years in the classroom. In fact, as a professor, I go back into public school classrooms to teach physical science units each year. I bring student teachers to observe and assist so that my practice is transparent and my reflection is visible. Sometimes we cringe when we go back to our beginnings, but if you are like me, you also remember the passion, energy, hopefulness, persistence, and curiosity.

Fearless Reflection

▶ This box and subsequent boxes are intended to help you begin to apply some of the ideas in the book with the hope that this will accelerate growth as you reflect, risk, revise or reject. Think of these boxes as the groundwork for the action steps at the end of subsequent chapters. Whether you are reading this on your own or with a group of educators, you have to be fearless in your honesty. Many of these boxes will ask you to rate yourself or others. Don't get hung up on the technical quality of the rating scales. These are not scientific, but are designed to force you to be honest and take a position so that you can reflect and grow.

On a scale of 1–10, how much value do you place on learning vs. knowledge?

- 1 = "Knowledge is all that matters."
- 10 = "Learning is all that matters."

| 1 | 2 | 3 | 4 | 5 | 6 | 7 | 8 | 9 | 10 |

Based on the notion that ten thousand hours of deliberate practice equals expertise, where do you fall on the expert novice continuum for teaching?

- 1 = "I have zero hours of deliberate teaching practice."
- 10 = "I have had ten thousand hours of deliberate teaching practice."

| 1 | 2 | 3 | 4 | 5 | 6 | 7 | 8 | 9 | 10 |

What are the implications of your view on learning vs. knowledge and where you fall on the novice-expert continuum?

IT'S NOT ABOUT "NOVICE" *INSTEAD OF* "EXPERT"

I am certainly not arguing that we should simply replace experienced teachers with new or unprepared teachers. In Wisconsin, legislation has been considered that would allow anyone, even a high school dropout, to be licensed to teach (Richards, 2015). This is not the novice to which I am referring, and I certainly do not want to romanticize being a novice. There are many drawbacks and challenges associated with being new to teaching, the most challenging aspect of which is the self-referential focus that makes it difficult to be fully aware of students. Sometimes, we refer to this as a teacher's "radar"—novice teachers can be so focused on what they are doing that they only see teaching and not learning. This is a significant challenge to overcome in addition to learning new curriculum, understanding the school and community culture, and figuring out how best to meet the needs of as many as two hundred individuals in the course of a day.

What I am arguing is that there are certain ways of thinking that novice teachers may demonstrate, out of necessity or naiveté, that some veteran teachers lose. Whether they are twenty-one-year olds or forty-five-year old career changers, novice teachers often demonstrate playful innovation, flexibility, and desperation born out of necessity and hubris that have distinct advantages in an ever-changing education landscape. These attributes are not unique to the novice but do seem to be more typical. This may be due to the fact that novice teachers do not know all of the reasons why an idea won't work. The knowledge of the many barriers in education can be one of the major constraints on my creativity as a twenty-year teaching veteran.

> Whether they are twenty-one-year-olds or forty-five-year-old career changers, novice teachers often demonstrate playful innovation, flexibility, and desperation born out of necessity and hubris that have distinct advantages in an ever-changing education landscape.

Many accomplished teachers maintain this playful innovation and are always experimenting, reflecting, and adapting. Because of their experience and deep understanding of teaching and learning, this can make them extremely effective. However, some veteran teachers lose this mindset and, in so doing, lose the joy and excitement of teaching. Novice teachers experience the exhilaration mixed with terror of learning alongside their students and with other colleagues. Over time, they can refine those innovations and make them better, but they should not lose their willingness to take risks.

THE NOVICE MINDSET

Stanford University Professor, Carol Dweck (2006), has researched and written extensively on the growth mindset and its implications for parenting, business, and education. Dweck asserts that we must move beyond a "fixed mindset" to a "growth mindset" when thinking about intelligence. If intelligence and ability are fixed, some people are smart and some people are not, some people are capable and others aren't, and there is nothing we can really do about that. If intelligence and abilities are fixed, then there is no reason to struggle and grow in our understanding and practice. If intelligence and ability are fixed, reflection on risk and struggle do not lead to growth because there is no real room for growth. In fact, even those of us who think we have a growth mindset may be limiting the growth of students because of underlying assumptions from a deeply rooted fixed sense of intelligence and ability with labels derived from tracking or special education status (Hattie & Yates, 2014). If these things are fixed, then most of us should just give up.

However, if we approach education from the growth mindset, there is hope for all of us. Struggle, risk, and reflection are welcome tools of increasing knowledge, skills, and intelligence. We are naturally curious, but how do we get students to think? In fact, cognitive scientist Dan Willingham describes thinking as unnatural for humans (Willingham, 2009). Teaching is an infinitely challenging task.

Since there are countless opportunities for novices to struggle, risk, and learn from mistakes, their greatest asset may be a particular type of growth mindset: the novice mindset. The novice mindset is the belief that we grow continuously through fearless, deliberate practice. This is an orientation toward growth that prioritizes risk, reflection, and revision while humbly seeking feedback and insight from a wide range of sources. The novice mindset allows us to get better at getting better. Accomplished teachers know that they never really arrive at great teaching—they are always refining their practice and have formally and informally honed their skills at getting better. The sooner we figure this out for ourselves and recognize that failure, creative struggle, and building on success are requisite components of improvement, the faster we will grow.

> The novice mindset is the belief that we grow continuously through fearless, deliberate practice.

FIXED TEACHING MINDSET	NOVICE TEACHING MINDSET
Struggle should be avoided.	Struggle is an opportunity for growth.
Risk is dangerous.	Risk is an opportunity to learn.
I know what I need to know.	I need to learn from others.
Compliance and fear drive my work.	Creativity and courage drive my work.
Every day is just another day.	Every day is another day I can get better.
Practice = experience	Deliberate practice = expertise
I receive feedback when I have to.	I seek feedback.
New challenges mean more work for me.	New challenges are opportunities to grow.
Teaching can become stale.	Teaching is never boring.
Change induces fear and should be avoided.	Change can be embraced if it is in the best interest of my students.

CREATIVE STRUGGLE

Teachers with the novice mindset embrace creative struggle to improve their deliberate practice. Creative struggle is a critical component of what we do. Sometimes creative struggle comes from failure that motivates us and can lead to innovation.

Thomas Edison changed the world by engaging in creative struggle for decades. As a student who probably dealt with Attention Deficit Hyperactivity Disorder, he was considered "addled" as a child. However, this energy made his creative struggle almost mythical. He would work assistants into the ground sometime going non-stop for twenty-four to thirty-six hours at a time. The light bulb, his most famous invention, allegedly went through ten thousand iterations before he settled on a workable solution. Translation: that is ten thousand failures.

Michael Jordan, the greatest basketball player who has ever lived, spent his entire career motivating himself through failure. His basketball career really started when he did not make the varsity basketball team his sophomore year of high school. In his Hall of Fame induction speech, Jordan talked about the guy who took his spot on the team. "Leroy Smith was a guy when I got cut he made the team and he's here tonight . . . I wanted to prove . . . to the coach that picked Leroy over me . . . you made a mistake dude."

Jordan was being inducted to the Hall of Fame and he was still talking about Leroy Smith.

Throughout his career, Jordan's creative struggle was fuel for innovation. After winning three championships, Jordan realized he could no longer continue to take the punishment of driving to the hoop constantly, so he developed one of the most potent turnaround jump shots in basketball history. He won three more championships.

> While most of us do not like to talk about failure or struggle—at least until we have succeeded—we can all identify with it.

While most of us do not like to talk about failure or struggle—at least until we have succeeded—we can all identify with it. Success does breed more success, but there is usually some form of failure that has accompanied or driven us to that success. Failure in fact is one of the exceptional cultural aspects of the United States. In some ways, American failure is the envy of the world. A piece in the *New York Times* describes the enviable culture of fearless failure that drives the U.S. economy. Silicon Valley's mantra of "Fail fast, fail often" signifies that

> The freedom to innovate is inextricably linked to the freedom to fail. In Europe, failure carries a much greater stigma than it does in the United States. Bankruptcy codes are far more punitive, in

contrast to the United States, where bankruptcy is simply a rite of passage for many successful entrepreneurs. (Stewart, 2015, para. 15)

I am not advocating haphazard risk taking and failure that might lead to market-driven improvement in education. When students' lives are at stake, we cannot treat them as the collateral of education's version of a failed tech start-up. I am advocating for teachers who continue to build expertise through disciplined, yet fearless, risk taking. "Disciplined risk taking" is bounded by reflection on the front and back end. Reflective teaching practice is not new, but sometimes, thinking like a novice is the most productive way to do this fearlessly.

Fearless Reflection

▶ On a scale of 1–10, how willing are you to enter into creative struggle?

- 1 = "Please give me a script to read my students."
- 10 = "I am energized by creative struggle and can't wait to give my students opportunities to struggle."

| 1 | 2 | 3 | 4 | 5 | 6 | 7 | 8 | 9 | 10 |

On a scale of 1–10, how strong is your growth mindset toward your students?

- 1 = "I don't want to teach my students anything new because I don't want to clutter their minds."
- 10 = "My current class of students has two future Nobel prize winners, a President of the United States, four Olympians, and three concert pianists."

| 1 | 2 | 3 | 4 | 5 | 6 | 7 | 8 | 9 | 10 |

On a scale of 1–10, how strong is your novice mindset toward your own teaching?

- 1 = "I am being required to read this book. I have no plans to get better."
- 10 = "I love to get better through setting goals, collecting evidence, getting feedback, and reflecting."

| 1 | 2 | 3 | 4 | 5 | 6 | 7 | 8 | 9 | 10 |

How might these three scores affect the way you read the rest of this book? How might they affect your students' learning?

A BRIEF LOOK AT THE CONDITION OF U.S. EDUCATION

Before we can really explore the various facets of the novice mindset, we must first explore the context in which they are applied. We have to understand the conditions in U.S. education to determine how to fearlessly embrace the novice mindset.

Nancie Atwell, a literacy guru and widely respected educator received the Global Teacher Award, a one million dollar prize for teaching. In an interview after receiving the award, she said, "Public school teachers are so constrained right now by the Common Core [State] standards and the tests that are developed to monitor what teachers are doing with them. . . If you're a creative, smart young person, I don't think this is the time to go into teaching" (Moeny, 2015).

While standards and testing do not have to stand in the way of creativity, many educators agree with Nancie Atwell. According to surveys (MetLife, 2012; 2013) of U.S. teachers, only 39 percent of teachers found their jobs "very satisfying" and 29 percent of teachers planned to leave teaching within the next five years.

39% of teachers found their jobs "very satisfying"

29% of teachers planned to leave teaching within the next five years.

(MetLife, 2012; 2013)

In many states, there is a growing narrative about teachers that they are actually overpaid, their pensions are exorbitant, and educators are a drain on the system as opposed to a benefit (Andrea, 2013; Costrell & Podgursky, 2009; Riddell, 2014). Since Thomas Jefferson, one of the most attractive aspects of teaching has always been that educators, while not particularly well compensated, are key contributors to a democratic society. While many still view teaching as a noble profession that provides a valuable service, this view appears to be eroding (for a very readable examination of the teaching profession over time, see *The Teacher Wars* by Dana Goldstein, 2014).

Furthermore, the accountability culture in U.S. public schools does not necessarily lend itself to risk taking and creative struggle. Teachers and students must be allowed to innovate which means they will have to take chances, collect data, get feedback, and reflect. In many organizations that privilege innovation, they encourage employees to "fail faster." Many districts have taken an approach that is antithetical to innovation. In these districts, there is talk of "teacher-proofing" curriculum and personalized online learning so that anyone can teach. This is not the fault of standards, Common Core, or otherwise. Standardized testing itself is not necessarily to blame, but is likely an outcome of this culture. There is a pervasive lack of trust that inhibits risk, creative struggle, and subsequent innovation.

Much of this is not new. Several sociological conditions hamper the novice mindset. First, lack of trust within schools is tremendously problematic for growth to occur in teaching and learning (Bryk & Schneider, 2002; Hattie & Yates, 2014). Without trust, little progress will be made within schools. Second, the "apprenticeship of observation" (Lortie, 1975) is another impediment to growth. Teaching is plagued by the notion that we all know how to teach because we have all been students. With this low view of teaching, informed innovation is difficult because there is a sense that we should just replicate models that we thought were effective as students and avoid the ones that did not work for us. This myopic view of improving practice can be extremely limiting.

Third, the egalitarian norms in teaching can be challenging for teachers. Many novice teachers bring an optimism and idealism to the work that they hope to do. Many of us entered teaching wanting to make a positive impact on the world. Somewhere along the way, many of us

> While the reality of the challenges we face in teaching is important to share, we must not crush the idealism that many novices bring.

begin to confuse reality with pessimism and see the idealism of novices as naiveté. While the reality of the challenges we face in teaching is important to share, we must not crush the idealism that many novices bring. One of the most unfortunate aspects of our profession occurs when veteran teachers try to convince bright, optimistic beginners that this optimism is naïve and misplaced. Being realistic is necessary but should never be confused with pessimism. I would much rather see a teacher who is overly optimistic than someone who believes reality dictates that teachers should be pessimistic about prospects for students. How often do beginning teachers hear the following kinds of statements from veterans in buildings they enter?

"Oh, you are just being idealistic. Just wait a few years."

"That stuff you learned in college is fine, but you don't really need any of that."

"That might work in some places but not here."

"This is the best job we can do with these kinds of students."

"Stop doing that. You are making others look bad."

"That is not part of our contract."

Watch what happens to a teacher when he or she is singled out for recognition or an award. In many school cultures, that teacher will be criticized, broken down, and ostracized. Daniel Duke (2008) describes this phenomenon with a crabbing metaphor. He calls it education's "crab bucket culture." A crab bucket does not need a lid because crabs will pull other crabs down if they try to climb out of the bucket. While teachers' actions may be subtler than this, when teachers stand out there is a pressure to pull them back into the mainstream.

Steps need to be taken to empower novice and veteran teachers alike to feel that they can move beyond their own individual classrooms while not necessarily leaving them behind. This includes simple steps like professional learning communities where true collaboration occurs. The novice teacher might be able to assist others in some of the technical aspects of instructional technology, while more experienced teachers can help the novice understand different aspects of the school community and effective, contextualized teaching techniques. This collaboration must occur within the bounds of nonevaluative, nonjudgmental, supportive norms where teachers see each other teach.

Systemically, differentiated, career lattices, hybrid roles, policy fellowships, and other leadership opportunities for teachers to spread their expertise are essential (Alexandrou & Swaffield, 2014; Berry & Eckert, 2012; Berry, Byrd, & Wieder, 2013; Lieberman & Miller, 2004; York-Barr & Duke, 2004). The most effective way to improve teaching and learning in schools is to increase deliberate practice. For that to occur, teachers need guidance, feedback, and time to reflect. That best occurs with other educators. This is a proposition that our current system does not seem to support based on the culture and structures in most schools. As teachers grow in their novice mindset and seek new challenges, opportunities and support must be available to continue to grow and expand their influence.

LOST OR TAKEN AWAY?

The novice's passion, energy, hope, persistence, curiosity, and creativity can be lost. They can also be taken away by systems that oppress and distrust teachers. Prescriptive teaching and "teacher-proofed" curricula do not create the conditions that will rid the system of ineffective teachers, much less catalyze innovation. The micromanaging of teachers that is occurring in many schools may minimally improve poor to average teachers, but it is driving good teachers out and is a deterrent to potentially talented teaching candidates from entering education as a career. The creativity of our students is the envy of the world. The best way to cultivate that creativity is by modeling it.

One of the strongest novice teachers I have ever seen, Marcey Wennlund, is an illustrative example of a teacher who is struggling against a system that lacks trust. In her first year of teaching in a third/fourth split classroom in a suburban Chicago public school, Marcey is attempting to meet the various needs of her students. She is an excellent reading teacher having worked under an outstanding mentor teacher. She has received proficient and exemplary ratings from her principal throughout her first year of teaching. On a weekly basis, multiple observers enter her room. This should be extremely beneficial to a novice teacher providing her in-depth feedback on her practice.

However, the feedback is primarily focused on the length of the varying components of her lessons. She describes the feedback she receives like this:

> You took four minutes on your lesson introduction and you should have taken three. You gave students thirty seconds to talk in the pair-share portion of the lesson, and you should have given them forty-five seconds. Additionally, when you have them partner share, you should assign partner #1 and partner #2. Partner #1 should speak the first time and partner #2 should speak first the second time. After they have shared, then you should recognize their effort with two snaps of your fingers.

This is not an environment that privileges innovation. Marcey is in a compliance-driven atmosphere in which very few creative, innovative teachers will thrive—novice or veteran. Unfortunately, this is the type of environment in which many educators currently exist. Environments like this can be particularly toxic for novice teachers and deadening for veteran teachers. However, this is not the state of every school, nor does it have to be. In fact we know that for schools to be successful, trust must be at the center of the enterprise (Bryk & Schneider, 2002).

Contrast Marcey's example with that of another first year teacher, Graham Schultze. Graham is a fifth-grade teacher, also in the western suburbs of Chicago. He was hired at the school where he student taught. Graham is a prime example of a backpacking, firewalking pioneer. While he was a student teacher, his principal, Chris Silagi, described the challenges that Graham faced.

> His fourth grade class had most of the boys who rode the bus to the school from government-subsidized apartments. He just connected well with them. In fact, I had gotten approximately thirty office referrals from the bus these students rode to school, so he began meeting weekly with the student ringleaders on the bus as well as visiting the bus daily before it left. During that month, we got one office referral.

Graham was hired to teach fifth grade at that same school. He requested each of the boys from that bus for his class. They have made tremendous gains academically and socially this year. His principal has given him the latitude to test innovative instructional practices and given him space to build relationships with his students. Each week, the class focuses on a different desirable character trait such as respect for others, compassion, or diligence. When these traits are demonstrated and identified by Graham or other students, students earn "skrilla" (class currency). Each Friday, students turn in their "skrilla" to Graham's alter ego, Jerry "Big Bucks" Wilson to determine who will be that week's "skrillionaire." With this much esteemed recognition comes a picture with Jerry "Big Bucks" Wilson that goes on the "skrillionaire" board and the privilege of keeping a Captain America statue on the student's desk for the coming week.

FIGURE 1.1 Graham with Skrillionaire, Quinn

This is not something that could be scripted. This is not something that would work for every teacher. That is the point. Graham is effective because he playfully innovates. The innovation is derived from necessity. Some of the innovative ideas will certainly fail, but he will reflect and then revise or reject. Importantly, so will his students. He has developed a classroom community where taking chances is celebrated and modeled. He is not worried about looking foolish or failing. He is a savvy teacher who is using a novice mindset.

FROM CRINGEWORTHY TO DESIRABLE

Whether we are novices or veterans, how do we employ the desirable characteristics of being a novice while not being cringeworthy? Rule #1: Do not worry about being cringeworthy. The examples I shared at the beginning of the chapter are certainly not desirable teaching practices. However, if we constantly worry about making mistakes and failing, we cannot succeed.

> Rule #1: Do not worry about being cringeworthy.

Each year, I made my elementary and middle school students memorize the following quotations so that true success was at the heart of our enterprise for that year. They had to stand in front of the class and recite them to each other—part of not fearing failure. These are good reminders for us as administrators, teachers, parents and human beings.

"I can't accept not trying."

—Michael Jordan

"There is no substitute for hard work."

—Thomas Edison

"Far better it is to dare mighty things, to win glorious triumphs, even though checkered by failure, than to take rank with those poor spirits who neither enjoy much, nor suffer much because they live in the gray twilight that knows neither victory nor defeat."

—Theodore Roosevelt

The final quotation captures the strength of the novice mindset, the novice that will be successful at least. Teachers employing the novice mindset cannot worry about failure. Our only concern should be the "gray twilight" where nothing is risked and nothing is gained. When teachers model this, students begin to live and learn this way as well. This book is devoted to avoiding the "gray twilight."

Figure 1.2 illustrates the basic premise of this book. Starting with a novice mindset (Chapter 2), we apply a process (Chapter 3), to practices (Chapters 4–7) that will allow us to continue to grow perpetually (Chapter 8). This is an iterative process that should inform and perpetuate itself over the course of our careers as we move toward expertise.

Fearless Reflection

▶ On a scale of 1–10, how would you rate the level of trust in your school and district?

- 1 = "No one trusts anyone."
- 10 = "Everything we do is predicated on trust."

School: 1   2   3   4   5   6   7   8   9   10

District: 1   2   3   4   5   6   7   8   9   10

How is the current climate in education affecting you and your school?

Is your experience more like Marcey's or Graham's?

What opportunities do you have to build trust, collaboration, and a stronger teaching profession by breaking down the crab bucket culture?

How would the novice mindset help?

FIGURE 1.2 The Iterative Theory of Action Production

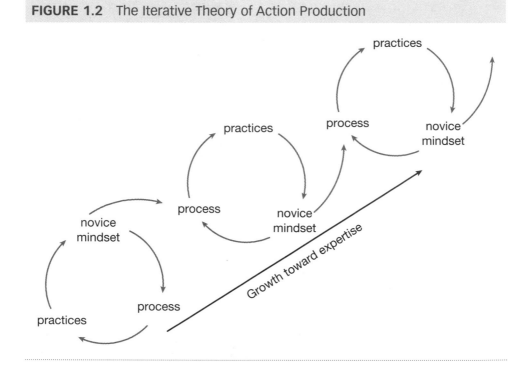

I hope you will embrace this work as we move away from the "gray twilight."

Key Takeaways and Fearless Practices

- The novice mindset is the belief that we grow continuously through fearless, deliberate practice.

- The novice mindset is an advantage as an expansive view of teaching. You can

  o acknowledge how little you know,
  o take chances,
  o seek advice,
  o see opportunities, and
  o cultivate a hopeful optimism.

- Given the rate of change in education and the fact that we are always meeting new students, we are all novices to some degree.

- In a "crab bucket culture" that lacks trusts and prioritizes compliance, you need the novice mindset.

- Whether you are a novice or veteran teacher, we can grow through transparent, deliberate practice.

- Find a setting where you can grow by taking disciplined risks.

- Don't worry about being cringeworthy.

- Avoid the "gray twilight."

Open-Ended Case Study

Let us return to Marcey, the first-year teacher from this chapter. In her context, she feels extremely constrained and limited in her ability to take risks. She is not receiving much support from her administrators that would really help improve her practice. She does have a small but growing network of colleagues in her building, district, former student teaching placement, and virtual connections through the Center for Teaching Quality. However, like all teachers, her time is extremely limited. What would you do if you were in Marcey's position?

Reflect

- What are the advantages of the novice mindset when approaching the current challenges in education?

- Who are some colleagues who display the playful innovation and energy of the novice mindset?

- How can you foster a novice mindset in yourself? In students? In colleagues?

- What steps could you take to move toward becoming an expert novice?

Risk: 3-2-1 Action Steps

3:   Identify three novice mindset strengths that you will develop or capitalize on this semester.

Possible Steps:

- Acknowledge how little you know—Seek out a colleague to learn from either inside or outside your building.

- Take a chance—try something bold.

- Cultivate hopeful optimism—identify an issue about which you have been negative. Think and speak about it in only positive terms for a week.

2:   Identify two colleagues who have a novice mindset and engage them.

Possible Steps:

- Talk to colleagues and identify others who seem to always be growing and improving.

- Take fifteen minutes to discuss with the two people you identify and try to implement one idea from each person this week.

1:   Identify one opportunity where you can push beyond your comfort zone to develop your novice mindset.

Possible Step:

- Tell a colleague you trust about a cringeworthy moment from your teaching. Reflect on what you learned. How can you continue to grow from this experience?

Revise or Reject

After taking a risk, determine what to do next. Was it worthy of revision or rejection?

☐ Reject   ☐ Revise

Write down a few notes about what worked, what did not, and what you might change.

CHAPTER 2

Embrace the Novice Mindset

"High performance isn't, ultimately, about running faster, throwing harder, or leaping farther. It's about something much simpler: getting better at getting better."

—James Surowiecki in
The New Yorker, November 10, 2014

Getting better at getting better. Many professions have embraced this seemingly simple notion. Professional athletes, for example, have embraced this notion with obsessive fervency. In the 1970s, athletes generally trained by getting in shape and practicing with their teams. Now every aspect of training is specialized. Every calorie, gram of protein, carbohydrate, and fluid ounce is recorded. Every bit of biometric data is analyzed. Athletes have experts with PhDs as their individual conditioning coaches and skills coaches. Football players are using goggles from Nike that cloud for tenth-of-a-second intervals in order to learn to focus their eyes in the midst of chaos. Players and coaches watch endless hours of film to improve (Surowiecki, 2014).

In the profession that makes all others possible, this notion has not always been embraced. Getting better at getting better means that we have to admit that we have specific needs for improvement—not in a generic sense, but in extremely specific, and transparent ways. These areas for improvement can be identified by data, peer review, thorough evaluation, introspection, or maybe just common sense. Once these areas of growth have been identified, we must determine strategies to improve—preferably strategies that have evidence behind them indicating that they might be successful. We must then implement those strategies and collect information on their effectiveness. Finally, we must reflect on ways we can continue to improve on an individual level. At the individual level, we improve as teachers. If this is implemented on a systemic level we have learning organizations predicated on continuous improvement (Smylie, 2010). This will lead to the high performance of individuals and the system. This chapter deals less with the processes and more with the mindset necessary to get better at getting better.

THREE EXEMPLARY "NOVICES"

There are many types of novices. Novices can be twenty-one-year-old student teachers, or wily veterans who continue to push into new experiences and practices. Novices can be career changers who might have deep expertise in a field and then turn to teaching when they realize teaching is the greatest job in the world. Even with all of their expertise and preparation in an alternative route or traditional program, they are now novice teachers.

> Getting better at getting better means that we have to admit that we have specific needs for improvement—not in a generic sense, but in extremely specific, and transparent ways.

To better understand the potential of the novice mindset, let me introduce you to three exemplary novices—the beginning novice, the expert novice, and the perpetual novice.

- The *beginning novice* likely fits your conception of a novice—an inexperienced, yet passionate and energetic new teacher.

- The *experienced novice*, a seeming contradiction in terms, has been teaching for many years, but has never lost that passion and energy while remaining in the same classroom.

- The *perpetual novice* has wanderlust for new challenges and has perpetually challenged herself outside of her comfort zone.

They represent the novice mindset in very different ways. You probably would not even recognize two of these teachers as having a novice mindset—they certainly would not describe themselves this way. However, like any good inquiry approach, let us examine who they are and then see what broader generalizations we can make about these novices. We will start with the most recognizable, the beginning novice.

The Beginning Novice

Karis Parker is a third-grade teacher in Kansas City. I had the privilege of working with Karis in our teacher preparation program. She maintained a 4.0 GPA, was an outstanding student teacher, and held herself and her students to high standards. The college where Karis attended is located outside of Chicago, but she was determined to teach in an urban school in Kansas City. Although she was already licensed to teach in Illinois and had completed our four-year education program, Karis applied and was accepted as a Teach for America (TFA) corps member. TFA is a highly selective program that draws motivated graduates from elite universities who usually have not been in education programs. She proceeded to complete the five-week TFA summer institute and was hired to teach third grade. Karis is an opportunistic learner who takes advantage of any and all resources to improve her practice. She knew TFA would lead to a job, provide additional preparation, support her across her first two years, and connect her with other highly motivated corps members. Karis might have been an effective beginning teacher without TFA, but she sought out the additional support that TFA could provide so she could be even better.

Anyone familiar with the accountability and assessment systems in most states know that third grade is where the pressure is quite intense. Third grade is typically the first year that students take state standardized tests and while the assessments are meant to measure learning from kindergarten through third grade, the third grade teachers feel the pressure acutely. In the districts where I worked, there were stories of third graders vomiting before tests prior to taking them—pressure that is inadvertently placed on them by teachers who feel the pressure from principals who feel the pressure from superintendents who feel the pressure from school boards or mayors who feel the pressure from state and federal policymakers. Many teachers avoid third grade for this reason. They feel too constrained by the assessments and the associated pressures. Third grade, it would seem, would be the last place that we would find an effective novice who would display the characteristics of a teacher who prioritizes growth through resilience, curiosity, and playful innovation.

However, over Karis's first two years of teaching, that is exactly what she has been. She improved her instruction significantly over those two years by examining the work her students were doing as a result of her instruction. In her formal observation debrief with her principal in her second year, he told her that she did a "fantastic job using data." In his perception, she was the most adept at this of any teacher in the school. While we work extensively on data analysis and assessment in our program, Karis continues to do this because she is able to identify students' strengths and weaknesses through examining the work they do. She continues to improve by analyzing student work and then acting on that analysis.

> Teachers continue to improve by analyzing student work and then acting on that analysis.

Not surprisingly, she is finding teaching to be a fascinating improvement process. In an email she wrote, "School in general is going well. Second year is a million times better than the first year—maybe a billion times better." This is not an unusual sentiment, but Karis's focus on improvement made her second year even more rewarding than her first.

This is the key to the novice mindset—continuous learning and reflection. Some teachers may teach for thirty years, but may be teaching their first year thirty times if they are not reflecting and growing. Those teachers remain novices, but not in the sense that is beneficial. The next two "novices" are thirty-plus-year teaching veterans who have maintained the novice mindset while becoming what I call "expert novices."

The Experienced Novice

Nancy Carlson may be the greatest teacher who has never received a teaching award. Nancy taught kindergarten through second grade over thirty years at the same elementary school in suburban Chicago. She taught two generations of students at her small, neighborhood elementary school. Imagine the gray-haired, grandmotherly, calm kindergarten teacher with bifocals perched on the end of her nose.

That is not Nancy.

She has dark brown hair, loves to host parties, go on cruises, has reading glasses representing every color of the rainbow, and has more energy than most twenty-one-year-old student teachers. Nancy has been described by other teachers in her building as "a force of nature." If you have been in a kindergarten recently, you will realize what a tremendous asset that energy is for a teacher. Over the course of nearly a decade, I observed Nancy's kindergarten classes on an almost weekly basis. During that time, I saw her introduce her students to science, math, and reading concepts as if this was the first time she had ever considered the notion. And then she would repeat that with her afternoon class that very same day. She marveled at the unique characteristics of each of her students and got to know each one and his or her family. This was particularly true for students with challenging backgrounds and learning needs. One particularly challenging student responded to her request to pick up a paper for her with the charmingly un-kindergarten-like response, "What's the matter with you? Your legs broke?" Through persistence and sheer determination, she worked with this student (and his mother) on respectful responses to adults and students and by the end of the year he was a vastly improved student and human being.

To better illustrate Nancy's ability to continuously learn about her students and the craft of teaching, here is a brief example. Each spring, as part of the "family living unit," a euphemism for the beginning of sex education, Nancy would lead her class in an "egg to chick" unit. This was always one of the most memorable units for students. The class would get eggs from a local farmer, incubate them and about three weeks later, most of the eggs would hatch into chicks. If you can possibly imagine a sixty-year-old woman being more excited and curious about when the chicks might hatch and the characteristics of these "oviparous" (a word I learned from Nancy's students) creatures, then you have a sense of Nancy as a teacher. By conservative estimates, over the course of her career she did this well over forty times for both morning and afternoon kindergarten groups, but like a great Broadway performer, each one of her classes thought this was her first time experiencing the miracle of chicken life. They thought the same thing when they performed a play of *The Enormous Watermelon*, tracked the crumbs of the Gingerbread Man through the school, conducted the egg drop, or met Zero the Hero. Even at the end of her career, she was making changes to adapt for Common Core Standards or different external pressures. Her

> Even at the end of her career, she was making changes to adapt for Common Core Standards or different external pressures. Her energy and joy were contagious.

energy and joy were contagious. This is a truly remarkable thing for a teacher who perfected her craft over a thirty-four-year teaching career.

The reason Nancy has never received a formal teaching award beyond her students and their parents believing that she is the best teacher ever, is that she has avoided them. She feared being singled out for recognition. Remember the "crab bucket culture?" Other teachers at the school described Nancy as "the glue" that made the faculty at her elementary school a "cohesive team." She organized the social events—parties, baby showers, and retirement celebrations. Individual recognition did not benefit the school as a whole and might have created disharmony among the faculty. Nancy said, "Individual awards are not why I teach, and I do not want other teachers to look at me differently because of an award." While this is an unfortunate perception of how other teachers might respond to well-deserved recognition, this speaks to Nancy's humility—a hallmark of the novice mindset.

The Perpetual Novice

Bobbi Ciriza Houtchens taught all over North America. She taught English to English learners and other high school students in the U.S. and Mexico over a career that has spanned nearly forty years. She taught in the migrant labor camps south of Miami, in Washington, D.C. public schools, a middle school in Oaxaca, Mexico, and for over twenty years in San Bernardino, California as a high school English teacher. She was also a Teaching Ambassador Fellow at the U.S. Department of Education. Her evolving novice mindset was very much informed and shaped by the diverse experiences and challenges that she sought out over the course of her career. She is a risk taker who does not fear failure. In turn, her students also take risks and accomplish far more than others would have thought possible.

Bobbi's teaching was informed by her mother's experience as an immigrant to the U.S. from Mexico City. Bobbi's U.S. Department of Education biography page, describes her mother's story and how it has influenced her work.

> Newly arrived from Mexico City, Houtchens' mother entered first grade speaking no English and was promptly escorted to the nurse's office, scrubbed down head to toe, and sprayed with insecticide. She was seated with the other new immigrant children in class, and insecticide was sprayed down the aisle that separated them from the rest of the students. Houtchens never wanted other students to suffer the cruelties that we sometimes commit in the name of education. (U.S. Department of Education, n.d., para. 2)

As a student teacher, Bobbi created her own program to work with English learners at a local middle school because her university could not find any teachers of English as a Second Language (ESL) at the secondary level. She was dismayed to find that her students had been placed in special education classes, which was the accepted practice at the time. This began her career as a groundbreaking novice who was unconcerned about convention or what might not be possible.

While Bobbi evolved in her expertise and saw patterns, opportunities, and new perspectives, she never lost her novice perspective.

When I first met Bobbi, she was at the U.S. Department of Education working in the Office of English Language Acquisition. She taught me to never ask permission. She would show up at major events on Capitol Hill or at think tank convenings and tell them who she was and her title at the U.S. Department of Education. These two pieces of information meant very little to event staff, but the way she said it, with the full weight of her persona behind it, got her into many events to which she was not invited. She did not stop with just entry into the event. On multiple occasions, I saw her become a full-throated participant, always advocating for her students.

While Bobbi evolved in her expertise and saw patterns, opportunities, and new perspectives, she never lost her novice perspective that allowed her to take risks, step out of her comfort zone, and be the kind of amazing teacher and advocate that she remains.

In reality, we are all perpetual novices because teaching is such a complex task of knowing content, understanding how to communicate that content pedagogically (Shulman, 1986), and using an array of interpersonal skills with potentially hundreds of students each year. We are always learning and will likely never achieve a complete sense of expertise because the skills and knowledge we need are too diverse to fully master. Remember expertise is domain-specific (Berliner, 2004; Hattie & Yates, 2014), and there are many domains to master in teaching. Even teachers whom I consider to be expert teachers never classify themselves as experts. Humility and our own expertise dictate that we will always have more to learn.

Fearless Reflection

▶ Are you a beginning novice, an experienced novice, or a perpetual novice?

What do Bobbi, Nancy, Karis, and many other great teachers have in common that comprises the novice mindset?

What are the markers that set them apart in their optimism, activism, and professionalism?

To better understand the markers of the novice mindset, let's return to elementary school.

NOVICE MINDSET MARKERS

Have you walked into a good elementary school recently? What about a good middle school or high school? How do you know it is a good school? My definition of "good" here is a school that can demonstrate that all students are learning and growing. There are markers of quality schools all around if you look. Some of them are tangible and others are intangible, but they are there.

Good elementary schools are some of the most positive places on earth. If you are feeling a bit down about societal, political, or personal situations, just visit a good elementary school. You will see a building that demonstrates pride of place that is maintained as a community anchor. You will see student work on display. A school secretary who can manage sick children, the intercom, teacher needs, administrator demands, and anyone that enters the office—the portal to the entire school—will greet you. Moreover, you will be greeted with a smile and if you have been there more than two or three times, likely by name. From the office you will enter bright, colorful, optimistic hallways where the possibilities of childhood line the walls.

Peek into a classroom and you will see groups of students engaged in learning with a teacher who is learning alongside them. Geoffrey Canada, founder of the Harlem Children's Zone, said, "When you see a great teacher, you are seeing a work of art." I would only add that when you see that teacher's students you are seeing multiple works of art that become a beautiful tapestry and testament to student potential and teaching gifts. The implicit message in good elementary schools is that everyone can learn and that learning is celebrated as we grow together. According to longtime superintendent Colleen Wilcox, "Teaching is the greatest act of optimism," and that is obvious in good schools.

The markers of quality middle and high schools are also recognizable—pride in school, student work, innovation, creativity, and student engagement are readily evident. Similarly, the markers of a novice mindset are observable and can be developed. These markers include hopefulness, persistence, resilience, curiosity, playful innovation, and opportunistic learning. Figure 2.1 illustrates the types of novices and the requisite novice mindset markers.

> Teachers who do not see ceilings for their students, but instead see opportunities where others see dead ends, can cultivate what once might have been naïve optimism into hopefulness rooted in observed success.

Nancy and Bobbi's examples demonstrate how this novice mindset is about far more than being a beginning teacher. In fact,

FIGURE 2.1 Types of Novices and the Markers of the Novice Mindset

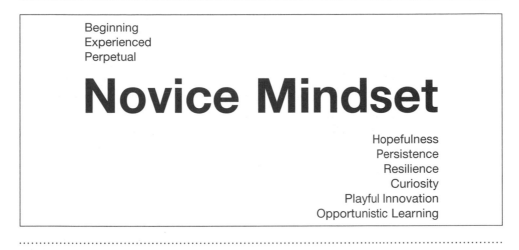

experts can demonstrate all of the markers and they can do so more clearly and efficiently. They see individuals, patterns, and opportunities with the wisdom that comes with experience. If they maintain markers of the novice mindset, they see all of these individuals, patterns, and opportunities with hope, curiosity, and nuance. If experience makes us more territorial, more willing to accept that this is the best that "these students" can do ("these students" representing a tacit lowering of expectations), more resigned to doing things as they have always been done, and more likely to believe that they have learned what can be learned, then we need to find a way back to the novice mindset. We want the teachers with novice mindsets at all stages of the career continuum. Teachers who do not see ceilings for their students, but instead see opportunities where others see dead ends, can cultivate what once might have been naïve optimism into hopefulness rooted in observed success.

The markers of the novice mindset are explored further below. At the end of the chapter, you will be challenged with ways to capitalize on these characteristics if you are a novice or veteran and already possess them. If you are trying to find your way back to these markers, there will be questions and action steps that will put you on the path back to the novice mindset.

Hopefulness

Most beginning teachers I work with enter teaching because they want to change the world. They may want to do this one relationship at a time, living life with a class of first graders, or meeting the needs of underserved students. Others want to completely transform the U.S. education system through education policy. Others

> If you are trying to find your way back to these markers, there will be questions and action steps that will put you on the path back to the novice mindset.

dream even bigger and want to alter the economic, social, and political structures that oppress underserved populations. There is an admirable, beautiful, maybe a bit naïve, optimism that makes me want to work with these beginning teachers.

As experienced teachers, we see shadows of ourselves in these beginning teachers. For teachers like Karis, Bobbi, and Nancy, the naïve optimism is replaced by informed hopefulness. They have seen students beat the odds. They have had students exceed all expectations. They have experienced the ways they have positively impacted the system, however great or small, which builds their sense of agency. Nancy and Bobbi have been able to experience this over the course of many years. They have not become jaded or cynical because they are grounded in hopeful experience that feeds their optimism. Their hope is based on an honest, unblinking assessment of what students have done and can do. Of course they get frustrated and would like to see the system change faster and more students succeed, but they choose to focus on growth instead of seeing the world as static, limited, or bleak.

Hopeful teachers are honest with their colleagues, students, and themselves. They look for and celebrate progress. Maybe a hopeful teacher remembered to submit his attendance to the office one day out of five in a week. He celebrates that day and thinks of the progress he can make. If he had one successful professional learning community meeting in a semester, he celebrates that one and tries to replicate it. These two examples may or may not have been something that I was able to experience growth with as a teacher.

Rita Pierson epitomizes the hopeful teacher. In her TED (technology, engineering, and design) Talk, "Every Kid Needs a Champion," she describes the type of teacher every student needs. Her approach is epitomized in a story she tells about a student's response to missing eighteen out of twenty questions on a quiz. She said:

> I put a 2 on the paper with a big smiley face. He said, "Miss Pierson is this an F?" I said, "Yes." He said, "Then why'd you put a smiley face?" I said, "Cause you on the road. You got two right." And I said, "You didn't miss them all and when we review this won't you do better?" (Pierson, 2013)

These examples represent incremental growth. However, we should not be afraid to celebrate amazing growth. Remember, we need to change the "crab bucket culture." If our students are doing amazing things, or even better if we see students doing amazing things with *other* teachers, we should identify that growth and celebrate.

Here are two observations of teachers who exude hopefulness: they never admit that they have bad classes, and they rarely "vent." For anyone who has been in a school as a teacher or even as a student, we have probably heard about a particular class or even entire grade level that is notoriously bad. In fact, we may have even been in one of those classes or grades. When we hear the group discussed, it is as if they are a school of piranhas that strip flesh from bone and leave nothing but destruction in their wake. Teachers dread the class, sometimes years before they arrive. When the students do arrive, the teachers and students are typically doomed to the logical outcome of self-fulfilling prophecy and confirmation bias. If we are trying to get back to the positive energy that we might have had as beginning teachers or maintain that energy, we cannot admit that we have a bad class—even if we have to lie to ourselves. There is no benefit in going down this road. We will only seek out confirmation of your assertion. Be deliberately optimistic (Silver, Berchemeyer, & Baenen, 2014).

Similarly, teachers displaying this marker of the novice mindset only selectively "vent." Venting is meant to allow us to release all of our negative feelings and energy about a subject. Many teachers think this is a healthy way to release tension about frustrating students, colleagues, parents, or administrators. Under the right set of circumstances, that assumption could be true. The best way to determine if venting has the potential to be helpful is to ask ourselves a few questions:

- What am I venting about?
- Who am I venting to?
- Did I seek this person(s) out because he/she will agree with me and confirm my anger and frustration?
- Is this person(s) likely to challenge my view or help me reframe the situation in a positive solution-oriented way?

The last two questions are the most important for determining if the venting will benefit others and us. Most of the time, when I vent I seek allies who will validate my "righteous" indignation. I do not want to be challenged in my views, and I walk away with my anger more firmly cemented, less hopeful, but feeling better because I am not alone. Schools can become toxic places for hope if venting becomes the norm.

> We need to stop venting unproductively and surround ourselves with people that challenge us to think differently and frame challenges positively.

Hopeful teachers do not do this. They rarely vent, and when they do, they want to be heard, and then eventually seek a solution. If we are trying to reclaim this hopeful optimism, we need to stop venting unproductively and surround ourselves with people that challenge us to think differently and frame challenges positively. If we are going to thrive, we cannot be people who incubate negativity and allow it to fester into professional putrescence. We need colleagues who will help us develop hopeful persistence and resilience. We also need to be those kinds of colleagues.

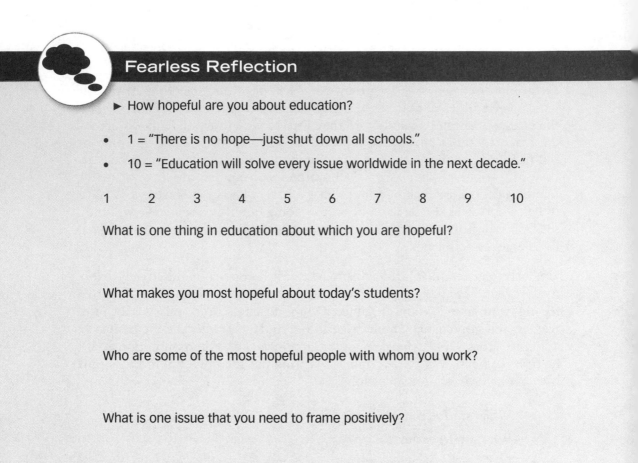

▶ How hopeful are you about education?

• 1 = "There is no hope—just shut down all schools."

• 10 = "Education will solve every issue worldwide in the next decade."

1   2   3   4   5   6   7   8   9   10

What is one thing in education about which you are hopeful?

What makes you most hopeful about today's students?

Who are some of the most hopeful people with whom you work?

What is one issue that you need to frame positively?

Persistence and Resilience

Over the last decade, "noncognitive skills" such as persistence and resilience have been identified as essential for students (Duckworth, Peterson, Matthews, & Kelly, 2007; Tough, 2012). We have all taught or been in school with students who are very bright, but are not motivated, or are easily discouraged. Many of these students become the dropouts, the glaring failures of the U.S. education system. Some of these students face great adversity at home, in their communities, or in school due to poverty, learning differences, language barriers, or myriad other challenges that students face today. However, some students facing these same challenges, sometimes against odds that seem insurmountable, succeed. Paul Tough (2012) has written eloquently about the role of persistence and resilience in the success of children. The noncognitive skill that seems to bubble to the surface as being of primary importance is grit—a combination of persistence and resilience.

Angela Duckworth and her team (2007) have been studying grit as an indicator of future success in various fields. Duckworth and her team have found that grit, as measured by their diagnostic survey, is the most important personal characteristic for determining potential. In their study of West Point cadets, for example, they found that the best indicator of likelihood of successful completion was the "grit score" that cadets earned when entering the Academy. This score trumped ACT, SAT, grade point average, physical fitness ratings, and any of the other data points that the Army collects on entry into West Point.

This does not surprise anyone who has taught. As a teacher, I saw students who were homeless show up to school every day. One homeless student, Kyle,[1] a waifish, blond-haired, fifth grader (think Charlie from *Charlie and the Chocolate Factory*) would show up some days hungry, exhausted, and emotionally fragile, but he would show up. He made great strides in fifth grade—strides that amazed even me. He grew as a reader, writer, mathematician, historian, and scientist. His confidence grew as he felt himself getting better at getting better. At the end of the year, Kyle and his younger brother moved to another city where their mother thought she could get a job. I lost touch with Kyle, but I believe Kyle's grit will lead to his future success. His story is not unique and is told over and over again in classrooms across the country. The question is how do we cultivate this in students?

The growth mindset has been well established for students. Dweck (2006) highlights the need for students to have the opportunity to struggle so that they will learn to persist. Failing well is a necessary part of risk taking. Students fail well when they take chances in a safe learning environment, learn from their failure, persist, and try again. They also succeed by building on successes that come from those failures. Success breeds future success. In Western cultures, we do not always value the struggle that typically leads to success—we value the success more than the process that leads to success.

In most classrooms in the U.S., we are not particularly comfortable with struggle. Our discomfort with struggle was illustrated beautifully by a National Public Radio story I heard driving in the car one day (Spiegel, 2012). Jim Stigler, a graduate student at the University of Michigan, was sitting in a Japanese fourth-grade math class. The teacher was teaching students how to draw three-dimensional cubes. One boy in the crowded classroom was having difficulty drawing this so the teacher asked him to draw his on the board. The rest of the class went on working, but every few minutes, the teacher asked the students to check to see if the student at the board had succeeded. This went on for the entire period. Stigler said, "I realized that I was sitting there starting to perspire because I was really empathizing with this kid. I thought, 'this kid is going to break into tears!'" The student continued to draw "with equanimity" until the end of class when his cube looked right at which point the entire class broke into applause and the boy sat down with an enormous smile on his face.

> Students fail well when they take chances in a safe learning environment, learn from their failure, persist, and try again.

---

[1] Pseudonym

Singling out a struggling student and giving him the opportunity to struggle publicly is perceived to be humiliating in most U.S. classrooms. In fact, we give less wait time after questions are asked and call on struggling students less in U.S. classrooms (Krueger & Sutton, 2001; Rowe, 1986). This is counterproductive for developing perseverance and resilience in our students.

Even the way we compliment our own children as parents and teachers discourages grit. What do parents say to a third grader when she comes home with 100 percent on a math test? Maybe something like, "Oh, I am so proud of you. You are so smart in math." Or what about when a child reads fluently and accurately? "You are such a great reader." On the surface, there may not appear to be anything wrong with this type of encouragement. However, the implicit message here is problematic when a child eventually struggles. If the child has been hearing for years that being "good" at something means understanding it quickly and easily, what does she think when she does not understand something quickly? "I must not be good at math anymore" or "I used to be a good reader." We need to be sure to compliment children and students on the hard work that they put into learning and stop attributing their learning to fixed personal attributes.

Intelligence is malleable, can be developed, and grows with increasingly challenging cognitive tasks. Intelligence is not a fixed entity that some people have and others do not. How do we help students understand this? How do we prioritize persistence and resilience?

A place to start is cultivating grit in teachers. We cannot just throw teachers into tough settings, tell them to be gritty, and then their students will succeed. I fear that this is sometimes the theory of action for many teacher preparation providers ranging from Teach for America to traditional teacher preparation programs. Beginning and veteran teachers alike need to be well grounded in the belief that they will continue to grow. Not only is this a realistic belief, this is a freeing one. Teachers will make mistakes, will teach lessons that can be improved, and they will continue to learn how to develop the pedagogical content knowledge (Shulman, 1986) that is a hallmark of effective teachers. When a teacher realizes that she does not need to be perfect, she is freed to pursue improvement.

There is a humility that should also accompany grit. Nancy, the kindergarten teacher highlighted earlier, demonstrated this in the way she focused on the needs of her students and colleagues. She did not ever make herself the focus of what was occurring at the school. Her students' growth was always the priority as she acclimated them to the school so that they would know that their hard work would take them as far as they wanted to go. This humility meant that she was willing to admit that she did not have all of the answers. This perspective made her an outstanding professional mentor to numerous student teachers and colleagues.

Sadly, in this era of accountability and testing, the willingness of teachers to admit that there are areas for potential improvement is sometimes inhibited by fear of reprisal. The willingness to be transparent about weaknesses also seems to decrease as teachers advance through their careers. Some veteran teachers believe that they must appear to have the answers and are not willing to invite others into their practice. Their doors close out of fear of judgment and a desire to protect their professional territory and hard won credibility. As in other professions, veterans stop taking chances, believing that they have found the answers that work for them. The problem with this is that sometimes veterans lose the ability to ask new questions and see things from new perspectives. One of the best ways to develop grit and create conditions where every teacher continues to grow is to emphasize curiosity and playful innovation in safe places.

Fearless Reflection

▶ You can go online and take your "determine your own grit" score based on Duckworth's work, or you can even more quickly determine where you think you fall on the scale below.

How persistent and resilient are you?

- 1 = "Just circling a number on this scale is exhausting."
- 10 = "Nothing can stop me. I am a teaching superhero."

1   2   3   4   5   6   7   8   9   10

How does humility influence grit?

Who are some of the most persistent and resilient people you know? What can we learn from them?

Curiosity and Playful Innovation

As a teacher of middle school science students, I was often asked how I avoided boredom when teaching the same labs four periods a day year after year. In other words, how did I remain curious and continue to innovate when the material did not seem to change? Like other teachers who are new to a curriculum or grade level, I had a novice mindset when I began. I was fascinated by the new science curriculum, our lab—students' first exposure in our district to a full lab, and the hormonal tempests that are seventh graders. As a novice, the question is how to make curiosity and innovation productive. As a veteran seeking to maintain a novice's mindset while growing in expertise, the question is how to maintain that fresh curiosity and playfulness.

For the novice, curiosity comes naturally and innovation is a necessity. There is a desperate need to figure out how best to serve students and a humility that comes with knowing that you do not have all of the answers. Getting to know students is novel. Those with a novice mindset find students, their backgrounds, and school culture fascinating because it is all new. The curriculum is new, the assessments novices use and design hold mystery for how their students will do. Determining ways to engage students, hold their attention, and tap into their prior knowledge is new. When students, curriculum, and assessment are all new, they can be overwhelming, but there is certainly no lack of curiosity. Beginning teachers need colleagues to come alongside them and space to analyze teaching and learning in a transparent, safe, and honest environment. Beginning teachers need time to reflect and examine these insights because the insights may be coming to them at a pace that does not allow for processing.

This curiosity can lead to experimentation. Many of the most successful companies in the world prioritize experimentation and playful innovation. Companies like Google and 3M require employees to take time away from their typical responsibilities to work on their own projects. In so doing, they are incentivizing creativity and problem solving. Unfortunately, this is not the case in most school systems.

One benefit of the novice mindset is that those who possess it are not constrained by all of the reasons why a new idea, bred from curiosity, cannot work. Bobbi's example is illustrative here. Her university could not find a secondary ESL teacher for her to student teach with, so she created her own program to work with middle school English learners who had been placed in special education classes. This is hardly ideal, but this kind of innovation benefitted not only Bobbi, but also her students. While many in education lament the current systemic issues, at least novices like Bobbi have helped us move past the unfortunate practice of conflating special education and English language acquisition.

Similarly, beginning teachers from around the country are innovating, sometimes in playful ways, even in what some perceive to be less than ideal circumstances. Karis has just started teaching in the height of the assessment and accountability culture in the eye of the storm—an urban third grade classroom. Her ability to learn and connect with her students in addition to her ability to understand and manipulate data has allowed her to successfully innovate and improve. Graham, the fifth-grade

> Coupled with grit, this type of curiosity-fueled innovation is the antidote to status quo, mediocre teaching practices.

teacher from Chapter 1, is playfully innovating to meet the needs of his students. He has developed his own class currency, numerous alter egos to teach things ranging from math to letter writing to character development. Coupled with grit, this type of curiosity-fueled innovation is the antidote to status quo, mediocre teaching practices. When grit and curiosity are combined, we find novices who are opportunistic learners.

Fearless Reflection

▶ How would you rate your ability to innovate productively?

- 1 = "I don't understand why we don't use workbooks for every subject."
- 10 = "Google would be lucky to have me."

1   2   3   4   5   6   7   8   9   10

What are the barriers to your curiosity?

What are your barriers to innovation?

What can you do to minimize those barriers?

What is an issue in education about which you are curious?

Opportunistic Learning

Effective novices in all fields are opportunistic learners—they have to be. They ask a lot of questions and cannot be concerned if there are stupid questions—they likely do not know enough to be able to identify if there are stupid questions. As they gain expertise, one of the best indicators that this is occurring is the quality of the questions they ask. Moreover, to make up for their lack of expertise, novices network with others to tap into the expertise located within these connections. Wiseman and her team (2014) found that novices significantly accelerated their learning curves by learning from and listening to others. When managers were asked what novices bring to their work, they most frequently answered, "openness." They did not bring a lot of new ideas—due to a lack of knowledge—but this lack of knowledge actually facilitates this openness.

Why does this openness diminish as we gain experience in our fields? Shouldn't we all be opportunistic learners? Maybe we are afraid. We are afraid to ask for help, or ask questions that make us look like we are dumb, or we think of all the reasons why something cannot work. As teachers, we know this is a terrible perspective for our students to have. Why do we let teachers think like this?

In addition to this fear, teachers also might not have the opportunities to learn from each other. Sadly, it is rare for teachers to be able to see each other teach, collaborate on specific lessons and strategies, and look at actual student work—not just color-coded test score reports. Teachers in other countries like Japan, South Korea, Singapore, Canada, and Finland spend far more time learning with and from one another. These countries have been described as "relentless" in their pursuit of teacher development (Jensen, Hunter, Sonnemann, & Cooper, 2014).

> Teachers with a novice mindset are those who need to harness the knowledge and experience of others.

Teachers with a novice mindset are those who need to harness the knowledge and experience of others. We need to develop our own Personal Learning Networks (PLNs). In order to ensure that PLNs do not just add more work to plates that are already full, this should happen through collaboration that is mutually beneficial. These PLNs can develop in person, within building, beyond buildings, and virtually. Figure 2.2 briefly describes the possible components of a PLN, and the next chapter explores the PLN in more detail.

FIGURE 2.2 Personal Learning Networks

Professional Library
- key research (e.g. ASCD SmartBriefs)
- reliable curriculum (e.g., LearnZillion)
- professional publications (e.g., The Reading Teacher, NSTA publications, Kappan, Educational Leadership, Education Week)
- blogs (e.g., Education Week Teacher, Larry Ferlazzo)
- idea generators (e.g. pinterest, teacherspayteachers)

Beyond School Colleagues
- district colleagues
- virtual colleagues (e.g. CTQ's Collaboratory)
- Professional organizations (e.g. ILA, NCTM, NSTA)
- former teachers, professors, and mentors

School Colleagues
- administrators
- specialists
- teachers
- para-professionals
- coaches
- secretaries
- custodians
- parents
- students

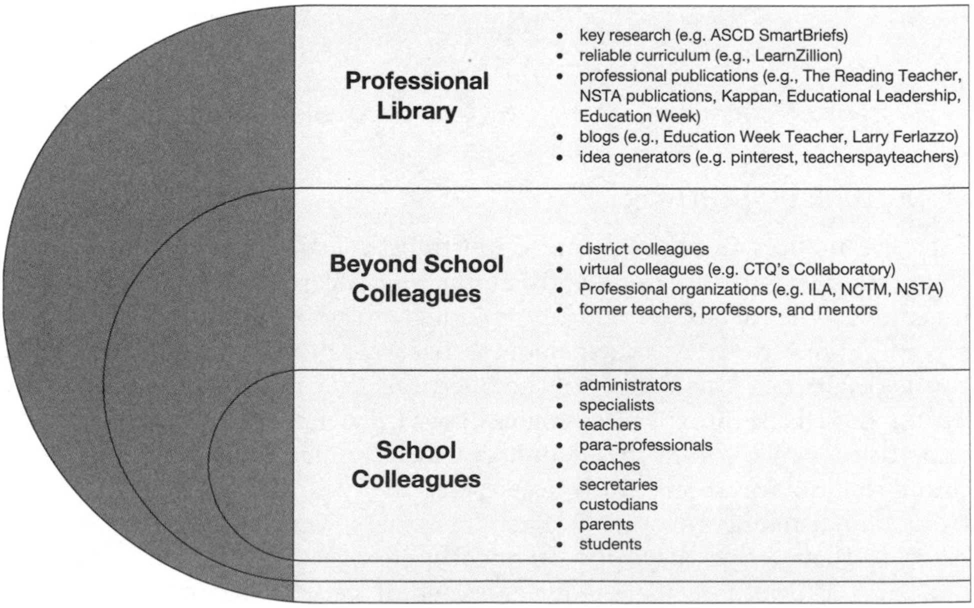

John Scheidt, an outstanding teacher, left the profession after fifteen years in the classroom and completing an EdD in School Leadership. He had lost his novice mindset. He is now a corporate headhunter. The joy of teaching was gone for him—he had lost his desire to persevere because he felt that his creativity, desire to learn, and drive to innovate had been wrung out of him by the system. "I don't miss it. I had lost the joy of teaching. The system no longer values wisdom and creativity. I felt like the system was boxing me in and the box kept getting smaller and smaller. I was suffocating." He echoed what I have heard from many teachers still in the classroom and others who have left. Many of the teachers still in the classroom who have expressed these sentiments would have left already if they had other options. John and other teachers have lost the joy that they once found in teaching. Much of this joy is predicated on a teacher's resilience, curiosity, and opportunity to learn—all of which have diminished over time.

Fearless Reflection

▶ How would you rate the strength of your PLN?

- 1 = "I consult with myself."

- 10 = "I have all the resources and colleagues I could ever need at my disposal."

| 1 | 2 | 3 | 4 | 5 | 6 | 7 | 8 | 9 | 10 |

What are the strengths of your PLN?

How could you enhance your PLN?

DEVELOPING AND MAINTAINING A NOVICE MINDSET

How do we ensure that Karis, Marcey, and Graham, the three beginning teachers who have been highlighted, cultivate their novice mindsets so that they get better at getting better?

How do they become experienced novices like Bobbi and Nancy?

At a minimum, how do they avoid burning out like John?

Just as great teachers create space for their students to grow, we need to create professional space for teachers to grow. The next chapter will address the processes associated with developing the mindset described in this chapter. However, in order to leave this optimistic chapter, I want to end with a quotation that one of my English preservice teachers, Justin Johanson, sent me after a class he took from me. He is working in one of the centers at our college to transcribe letters from the writer and poet, Dorothy Sayers, to her mentor, Charles Williams. She wrote, "Nothing so makes the pupil expand as the teacher's generosity of welcome which makes them feel more brilliant and original than they are" (Reynolds, 1998, pp. 78–79). The quotation encapsulates the essence of what the novice mindset is for teachers and students. We must extend this "generosity of welcome" to our students, ourselves, and each other as we improve as teachers. This improvement is fueled by the systematic process described in the next chapter for getting better at getting better.

Key Takeaways and Fearless Practices

- Get better at getting better through honest reflection and transparent practice.

- Be a beginning, experienced, or perpetual novice.

- Demonstrate hopefulness, persistence, resilience, curiosity, playful innovation, and opportunistic learning.

- Your hopefulness is rooted in idealism and can be developed through honest assessment of progress.

- Do not condition expectations for "these students"—do not see ceilings.

- Never admit you have a bad class.

- Seek out people that will help your reframe problems and find solutions.

- Make room for curiosity and playful innovation by focusing on what could be possible.

- Observe others, find mentors, and develop your personal learning network.

Open-Ended Case Studies

Select one of the teacher case studies below and answer the associated questions.

- Graham is just finishing his first year of teaching fifth grade. How might his novice mindset have helped him be successful in his first year? What will he need to do to cultivate that mindset in his second year? What will he need to protect himself against in order to maintain hope, persistence, curiosity, and his desire to learn and innovate?

- Karis is now a third-year teacher in a new school but still teaching third grade. How can she use her novice mindset to benefit her new school and students? What obstacles might she face in a new building? How will being in a new school benefit her novice mindset?

- Nancy is now a student-teaching supervisor and long-term substitute teacher. How can she use her novice mindset to benefit her student teachers? How might she have benefitted you as a beginning teacher? What are three things she can do to continue to hone her novice mindset as someone who has been an expert teacher for many years?

- Bobbi is still teaching—sometimes students, but now more often as a professional development consultant. How can she use her novice mindset to benefit the profession in this new role? What aspects of Bobbi's experience were particularly valuable to her novice mindset?

Reflect

- What do you do to remain hopeful about students, teaching, and education?

- What do you vent about and to whom? Why do you vent to them?

- What role have persistence and resilience played in your professional journey?

- What is one innovation you could try in your classroom this week?

- What is one learning opportunity that you could take advantage of in the next month?

Risk: 3-2-1 Action Steps

If you have not already, complete each of the scales in this chapter and total your score.

Total: _____ / 40

This will give you a sense of how strong your novice mindset is. Unless you scored a 40, we all have room to grow. Then . . .

3: Identify three areas where you think you could be more hopeful and persistent. Take an honest assessment of where you stand as a teacher and what you believe about your students. Identify areas where you could increase your expectations for yourself and your students.

Possible steps:

- Stop unproductive venting.

- Track the student successes you are seeing.

- Highlight for students where you have seen their persistence pay off.

- Identify and encourage a colleague doing quality, unnoticed work.

2: Identify two learning opportunities that you and a partner or a team at your school could try this semester.

Possible steps:

- Agree to reciprocal observation—where you agree to observe one another—tell your principal you will need two hours this semester to do this. If you are a principal reading this, make this happen for your team.

- Develop your PLN (e.g., by joining or subscribing to the Association for Supervision and Curriculum Development (ASCD) Smartbriefs, joining something like the Center for Teaching Quality's Collaboratory, or learn one thing from another teacher outside of your building.)

1: Identify one innovation that you and a partner or a team at your school could try this semester.

Possible steps:

- Create a new assessment that measures students' skills or knowledge that you think are important.
- Try out a new questioning strategy of classroom management technique. Can't think of anything? Keep reading, or ask another teacher.

Revise or Reject

After taking a risk, determine what to do next. Was it worthy of revision or rejection?

☐ Revise   ☐ Reject

Write down a few notes about what worked, what did not, and what you might change.

CHAPTER 3

Reflect. Risk. Revise or Reject.

"Ingenuity is often misunderstood. It is not a matter of superior intelligence but of character. It demands more than anything a willingness to recognize failure, to not paper over the cracks, and to change. It arises from deliberate, even obsessive, reflection on failure and a constant searching for new solutions."

Atul Gawande, from *Better: A surgeon's notes on performance* (2007, p. 9)

N o one wants to admit when they have made a mistake—especially not a surgeon. That is what makes Dr. Gawande's statement so remarkable.

He opens his book with an example of himself as fourth-year resident on his final year in medical school prior to becoming a surgeon. He had a patient who was having symptoms that seemed to indicate a common form of pneumonia. Her condition remained roughly the same for several days while on antibiotic. Then one morning during seven o'clock rounds, she complained of insomnia and sweating overnight. The senior physician overseeing Gawande told him to keep a close eye on her. Gawande planned to check on her again at noon. The physician, not trusting a medical student in his final rotation, checked on the patient twice that morning. He found that her oxygen levels were decreasing, temperature was rising, and blood pressure was dropping—all signs of a body shutting down. By the time Gawande checked on her at noon, he found her already under treatment for septic shock and recognized that the senior resident had saved her life.

This recognition of the senior physician's actions and his own error led Gawande to write *Better: A surgeon's notes on performance*. In the book, he describes what is required for surgeons to get better at what they do. He asserts that getting better is dependent on diligence, doing right, and ingenuity. Certainly, as patients this is what we want from our doctors. This is what our students want from their teachers and administrators as well. In medicine, lives are always at stake. While that might not be the case on a daily basis for a teacher, we know that our students' lives and future success are also on the line. That is why there is urgency for us to continue to grow. His definition of ingenuity is particularly helpful in relation to the processes associated with getting better at getting better. He highlights the importance of reflection, admitting when you have failed, and finding solutions that will lead to better performance.

In the most viewed TED talk ever, "Do schools kill creativity?" Sir Ken Robinson asserts, "If you are not prepared to be wrong, you will never come up with anything original. . . . We are educating people out of their creative capacity." This is an indictment of education that begins with our risk-aversion that is derived from a fear of failure. This is sadly evident in teachers and students and does not seem to have gotten much better since Robinson's speech in 2006. If creativity is as Robinson describes, "Having original ideas that have value," then schools are in trouble. If schools are not facilitating creativity, then society is in trouble.

I have had many, many opportunities to revise and improve upon almost every failure I have had in my classrooms—please note the emphasis on many. However, sometimes my learning from failure consists of rejecting the idea and never doing it again. I have had some clunkers that are best just forgotten. There is no shame in that—sometimes we take risks and those risks result in spectacular failure. Let me briefly illustrate with two spectacular failures.

Family Living

"Family Living" was a rite of passage for fifth graders in the district where I first started teaching. "Family Living" was the euphemism we used for "Sex Ed." As a first-year teacher and as the only male fifth-grade teacher, I had all of the fifth-grade boys in my room for the last hour of the day to watch our "Family Living" video, distribute deodorant, and leave time for questions and answers. I thought I could cut off the questions, by handing out the samples of Old Spice deodorant and focusing on personal hygiene. If you have ever spent time in a warm fifth-grade classroom and smelled the musky humanity, you will understand this need. I would have the boys repeat after me, "Deodorant is my friend."

After previewing the video, I really started dreading the day. The video was a dated piece from the 1980s featuring an older brother talking to a younger brother about the changes that would come with puberty. The primary focus of the video seemed to be about nocturnal emissions. Included in the video were animated diagrams of what occurs during these nocturnal events complete with arrows indicating the direction of the emission. I was a twenty-one-year-old guy, and I really did not want to talk to a large group of eleven-year-old boys about nocturnal emissions. I was extremely hopeful that the video would answer all of their questions.

Unfortunately, the video seemed to raise more questions than it answered. So I told them to raise their hands if they had questions.

At this point, any of you who have led one of these exercises knows that we are about to go directly off the rails. There was one student who looked particularly troubled. Fearfully, I called on him. He stammered nervously, "Does it really come out in arrows?"

I had to keep a straight face and answer this earnest question from a student who, based on his expression and concern, feared injuring himself in the night. About half the boys were snickering, and the other half sat uncomfortably wondering if this was a new horror of puberty that they should also fear.

The Lava Lamp

In my eleventh year of teaching, I decided my students needed a better understanding of how temperature affects density by making a "lava lamp" out of a Bunsen burner, ring stand, flask, and a couple of flammable liquids. You probably see where this is going and are wondering why I did not see where this was going with what should have come from eleven years of experience—if common sense was not enough. As the flask heated up, the two liquids began to demonstrate what happens when temperature decreases the density of a liquid as bubbles of the oil rose through the alcohol. For some reason that defied any understanding of science and pressure, I put a rubber stopper in the top of the flask. Just as third period was ending and students were exiting the science lab, walking by my lava lamp on the demonstration station, the stopper shot out of the flask, bounced off the ceiling, as alcohol and oil cascaded down the sides of the flask immediately igniting the entire surface of the demonstration table with flames reaching nearly to the ceiling. A student ran out of the lab yelling, "Mr. Eckert set the lab on fire! Mr. Eckert set the lab on fire!" up and down the hall.

The container of water from a previous demonstration proved to be very useful.

Upon reflection, flammable liquid + rubber stopper + flame = epic failure. There may be some shame in this circumstance given my status as science teacher who should have known better, but in most instances, we just need to acknowledge that something is not working and move forward. Needless to say, I have not made any more lava lamps.

Dr. Gawande's emphasis on learning from failure by acknowledging it and then searching for new solutions is particularly helpful for those operating from a novice mindset. In order for this mindset to produce improved teaching and learning, a four-step process is required. We will refer to these steps as the "Four Rs."

THE FOUR Rs

The Four Rs are: reflect, risk, revise or reject (See Figure 3.1). In formulating this, I struggled with which "R" should come first. Much of what novices do is haphazard risk taking because they are merely trying to survive minute-to-minute and hour-by-hour. Sometimes these risks result in amazing breakthroughs; however, this is the exception rather than the rule. Our reflection should inform our risk taking. For example, in my second year of leading "Family Living" talks, I had students write their questions down on notecards and submit them anonymously so I could filter them and compose myself prior to answering. The reflection may be a brief realization that a lesson is not working, but we have to identify the need we are addressing before taking a risk. This could be as simple as recognizing that we are doing too much of the talking and redirecting our class to more collaborative group work—or deciding that we need to enliven our discussion of density with a flammable lava lamp.

This model is a structured way to think about risk and reflection with a number of ideas to make this an iterative process. We do this already—we just need to be sure it is intentional and as well informed as time allows.

After taking the risk, we return to reflection to determine if we should reject (e.g., no more lava lamps) the idea or revise it (e.g., notecards for "Family Living" questions) for what is next. There is no shame in rejecting an idea. We should not defend an idea that should be scrapped. The good news is that most of the time there is something that can be salvaged. We need to identify if it was a bad idea, bad execution, or both. Upon reflection, some aspect of the idea will be redeemable and should make you a better teacher because of the experience. That revised idea leads to further risk taking and the cycle continues, all the while informing and being informed by the reciprocal nature of a personal learning network (PLN).

If we identify a more significant need that will require a more significant change, we should spend more time considering our options. Depending on the size of the risk, we should inform our reflection with our PLN. This PLN is not a new acronym for the sake of adding to the educational acronym alphabet soup or just another phrase for professional learning community (PLC). A PLN is vitally important for the very reason that PLCs have become another dreaded acronym that represents the educational idea du jour that everyone is in favor of theoretically but has gone terribly wrong in their implementation. While certainly not the case everywhere, something as positive as a professional learning community, something that teachers would seemingly all favor, is viewed by many educators as another attempt to control teachers and consume time through bureaucratic processes. This speaks to the need for teachers to inform their own practice through a variety of resources. As Figure 3.1 illustrates, the PLN is composed of your school colleagues, colleagues beyond your school, and your professional library.

Before objecting to the PLN or lumping it in with PLCs, give the idea a chance—you may be surprised how many resources you already have at your disposal.

> The PLN is composed of your school colleagues, colleagues beyond your school, and your professional library.

FIGURE 3.1 The Four Rs of the Novice Mindset

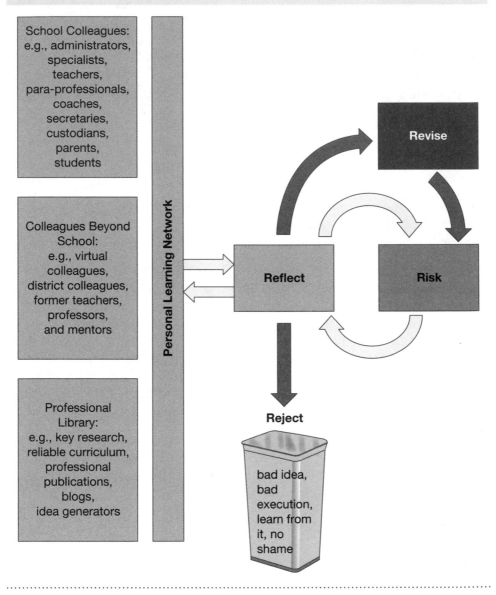

PLNs versus PLCs

Both PLNs and PLCs can have tremendous value. They are just different. The chart below provides a quick comparison to clarify each one.

PLN	PLC
• Self-directed	• School/administrator directed (can sometimes feel like "top-down" management)
• Focused on individual's goals	• Focused on school-wide goals
• Can be engaged at any time	• Meets at a given time
• No prescribed structure	• Uses protocols and has a reporting mechanism
• Can extend to colleagues and around the world	• Typically limited to colleagues within a school

REFLECTION AND YOUR PROFESSIONAL LEARNING NETWORK

As teachers, we know two things:

1. We are always learning
2. There is never enough time

Building a PLN needs to enable us to maximize learning while minimizing time. Here are a few ideas that might help. *This is not one more thing to add to your to do list*—"Get PLN." These are suggestions to make your life easier and to take advantage of resources that are readily available.

School Colleagues

We now know that collaboration is related to student achievement and that teachers who engage in better quality collaboration have better achievement gains in math and reading and that teachers improve at greater rates in these schools. To illustrate, in a study of over nine thousand teachers over two years, almost 90 percent of teacher reported instructional teams as "helpful" or "very helpful." In schools where collaboration was viewed more positively, student growth in reading and math increased at a higher rate than schools that were less collaborative (Ronfeldt, Farmer, McQueen, & Grissom, 2015). So why don't we ever get enough time to learn from each other?

I started teaching in a school with movable walls. There was noise from the library and the two adjoining classrooms. There was the noise from my room that traveled, almost without obstruction, into the other rooms. As teachers, we were aware of what was going on in others classrooms, but we never actually had the opportunity to observe or receive feedback from each other. We need reciprocal observation where we can see each other teach in a nonevaluative way. There is untapped expertise in every school building when there are not opportunities to examine practice and share ideas. Don't forget to enlist the help of office staff and custodians to understand the community in which the school is situated. In my experience, they have a deeper understanding of certain aspects of the community than almost anyone else in a given school.

> There is untapped expertise in every school building when there are not opportunities to examine practice and share ideas.

If we have had collaborative partners, we know how rewarding that work can be. Daniel Kahneman describes the collaboration that led to his Nobel Prize in economics. "The pleasure we found in working together made us exceptionally patient; it is much easier to strive for perfection when you are never bored. Perhaps most important we checked our critical weapons at the door" (2011, p. 6). While we might not end up with Nobel Prizes, we might end up with more rewarding work and better results for students if we can grow with our colleagues in nonjudgmental ways.

Beyond School Colleagues

Some of us teach grades or subjects where we are the only teachers. I have found it very difficult to learn with others when there is not mutual benefit. I am happy to help a sixth-grade teacher get better at teaching social studies students, but I am much better and more interested in talking to others who teach science to seventh graders. There are online communities that allow all teachers to find others who will derive mutual benefit from interactions about policy, research, and practice.

Another asset to having colleagues beyond your building in your PLN is that you can receive third-party feedback from knowledgeable, more objective outsiders. Sometimes this will be a new way to do something in your class that has not penetrated the practice of others at your school. Sometimes this will be a sounding board for ideas from people without a vested interest in how this will play out in your school. These colleagues can consist of professionals from around the world, professors, and former mentors.

> Sometimes this will be a sounding board for ideas from people without a vested interest in how this will play out in your school.

Professional Library

When I first started teaching, one of my mentors, Priscilla Lane, would arrive at my door three weeks prior to any unit with a binder containing all of the materials we would need for the upcoming unit. She told me, "The most important thing for a beginning teacher is organization." Without it, it is difficult to get better because reflection is hampered. I thought she was miraculous—her expertise and generosity certainly made me a better novice. She was the primary component of my PLN. We need much more than binders from mentors to thrive in teaching today.

> Become a critical consumer and find what works for you. Don't do more—just keep track of what you do so that you can more easily access it later.

Whether you use a wiki, a Google doc, website, or a tool like Zotero or Endnote, you need to start organizing the research, articles, and curricular supports that are important to you. We are professionals and professionals use research and data to inform what they do. Become a critical consumer and find what works for you. Don't do more—just keep track of what you do so that you can more easily access it later. This is smarter time, not more time.

The bigger the risk, the better informed it should be. Then we must leap. We cannot be paralyzed by fear of failure. Sometimes we will fall miserably short, but without taking risks and then reflecting on the results of those risks, we cannot grow. Occasionally, we will completely reject the innovation based on its outcomes (e.g., flammable lava lamps); however, most of the time we can learn something from the result. Then we revise our efforts and try again. As good members of our PLNs, we should share our results with our network. By doing this, we have the potential to improve the practice of other educators through this iterative process. If we do not apply the Four Rs, we have the potential of teaching our first year for thirty consecutive years. By sharing what we learn, we help others grow as well.

To illustrate the Four Rs, let's examine how they work in the classroom.

THE FOUR Rs TRANSFORM THE CLASSROOM INTO AN EXPLORATORIUM

If you have never been to the newly redesigned Exploratorium on the piers in San Francisco, then you need to go. If for any reason you are laboring under the misapprehension that humans do not like to learn or do not like science, then you have not been to the Exploratorium. When they can wrestle the displays away from parents who want to play, there are hundreds of interactive displays that allow children to test out nearly every physical science concept imaginable. From giant sheets of soap bubble film to becoming human components of experiments in potential and kinetic energy, children are engaged in reflection, risk, rejection, and revision. In the center of the Exploratorium, you can watch scientists and engineers designing future displays.

> Is it possible in this accountability era to have classrooms that prioritize reflection and risk taking?

Fearless Reflection

▶ Take a few minutes to determine how you can grow your PLN. Fill in the plan below:

My PLN

	Who and what are currently part of my PLN?	Who and what do I need to add?
School Colleagues		
Beyond School Colleagues		
Professional Library		

What if our classrooms were like this? Is it possible in this accountability era to have classrooms that prioritize reflection and risk taking? How can we find the freedom to model this kind of exploration of what works for our students? Reflection with evidence is certainly essential in this culture, but that is a hallmark of good exploration.

Fearless Reflection

▶ Take a minute right now to begin thinking of your classroom this way and apply the Four Rs:

Reflect: What is my most urgent challenge? You cannot fix everything at once and you certainly do not need to overthink everything. If it is your most urgent challenge and will require some significant changes, you should certainly engage your PLN. Be sure to include people who think differently than you in order to avoid the echo chamber that can come with social media or only engaging people in your building. There are tremendous resources available online for curricular, professional, or classroom management issues. For example, Larry Ferlazzo, an accomplished blogger and curator of good content, lists all kinds of resources for teaching English learners on his site. LearnZillion is a group dedicated to posting an entire online curriculum in mathematics and English language arts. The lessons include embedded formative assessments that track student data and the number of downloads to determine the most useful and impactful lessons. Another tremendous asset to both of these sites that all teachers love—these resources are entirely free.

Risk: After you have spent some time reflecting on, discussing, or researching your challenge, what will you do? You identified it as a challenge so remaining with the status quo is likely not an option. You are going to have to do something differently. What is it that you will do and how will you know whether it benefited your students? If you are taking a calculated risk, then you need to be sure to calculate its impact as well.

Revise or Reject: Assess what did or did not work, formally, informally, or both. Remember that every student is different, so therefore every class will be different, so there will always be opportunity to experiment. Always be sure to capitalize on and share your successes, but also, share your failures. Embedded in our human nature is the fact that we resonate with struggle. Humbly sharing your failures will model the kind of transparent embrace of struggle that we want for our students and profession.

The remainder of this book is devoted to applying the novice mindset and these processes to practices that will allow us to better serve students. The practices are not comprehensive, and you will not miraculously become a great teacher if you just do what these chapters prescribe. You will find some practical things to take away from the coming chapters, but the approach is far more important than the actual practices. If you are like most of the teachers with whom I have worked, the ideas in the following chapters will do one of two things for you:

1. Some of the ideas will resonate with you and reinforce some things you are already doing.
2. Some of the ideas will challenge you to think differently about our practice and profession.
   a. You will reject some of these ideas as being unrealistic, idealistic, or naïve.
   b. You will try to apply some of the ideas and then you will go through the final three Rs. You see, the fact that you are reading this book indicates that you are already reflecting. What is left is to risk, reject, or revise.

Teaching is complex and personal. Parker Palmer writes, "Good teaching cannot be *reduced* to technique. Good teaching comes from the *identity* and *integrity* of the teacher" (*italics* added for emphasis, Palmer, 2007, p. 17). Techniques are important and Palmer does not under-value them here— "reduced" is a very important word here. Some would argue that high leverage strategies (Ball & Forzani, 2011) or techniques (Lemov, 2010, 2015) are what matter most. However, if we emphasize this to the extent that the "identity and integrity" of the teacher are marginalized or irrelevant, we reduce teaching to technical reproduction. This robs teaching of joy, creativity, and reflective risk taking. There are signs that this is occurring in classrooms across the United States (MetLife, 2013).

We have to make a case for a profession that prioritizes a novice mindset and realistically applies reflective risk taking. To illustrate how this could positively impact teaching and learning, let's consider two common issues.

How Can I Express Who I Am in the Classroom to Improve Learning?

Spend a few minutes reflecting on these three questions:

1. How are you unique as a teacher?
2. What makes you different than other teachers?
3. What works for you when you work with students that might not work for others?

Do not misread what I am proposing here. There are certainly many common practices that work well for all teachers and should be used to some extent by all teachers. However, one of the biggest mistakes I see beginning teachers make is trying to be like their favorite teacher. There are a number of fallacies in this type of thinking.

1. That teacher was an effective teacher for other students.

2. As a student, I represented all students.

3. As teachers, we have decided that we like teaching well enough to spend our careers in schools therefore our students feel the same way.

4. All students will be inspired the way I was if I can replicate that teacher's techniques and persona.

5. That I can be that teacher.

Stop trying to be someone else. You cannot do that effectively. Yes, you can beg, borrow, and steal ideas—I may not have ever had a truly original idea in my nineteen years of teaching—but you have to be who you are. When you do something that truly comes from who you are as a person and it works for students in your classroom, you will feel that "spark between souls that no other profession can match."

> When you do something that truly comes from who you are as a person and it works for students in your classroom, you will feel that "spark between souls that no other profession can match."

An outstanding National Board Certified Teacher early childhood teacher, John Holland, shared that beautiful quotation with me several years ago as part of a professional collaboration session.

In pursuit of that "spark between souls," take a risk by embracing being quirky. We have to find what works for us in the classroom. One of my mantras for my middle school students was, "'Quirky' and 'weird' are far more interesting than 'normal.'"

One of the quirkiest people I ever worked with was our school custodian, Bob Santucci.[1] Bob was a Chicago guy in every way you can imagine. With a bushy mustache, salty mouth, and affable personality, he added a dose of local color to our neighborhood school. Bob's favorite word was "smooth." In Bob's thick Chicago accent, this sounded a lot more like "smuth" and seemed to emanate from beneath his mustache without his mouth moving. He could answer almost any question with the one word answer, "Smooth."

Me: "How was your weekend?"

Bob: "Smooth."

Me: "How are you feeling today, Jim?"

---

[1] Pseudonym

Bob: "Smooth."

Me: "Could you help me move those tables to the back of the library?"

Bob: "Smooth."

A student teacher and I came to very much appreciate Bob and his succinct form of communication. We began to use "smooth" as the highest form of general praise for our students. If they did well on a test, essay, or lab packet, instead of writing "Great job" or "Well done," they would receive our highest commendation: "Smooth." Just yesterday, I posted, "smooth" on one of my former student's Facebook page in response to a newspaper article that he had just published. I taught him thirteen years ago, but that one word still connoted high praise.

When I moved to Tennessee to teach in a middle school, the legend of Bob Santucci moved with me. Although my students had never met him, they soon became familiar with "smooth." In fact, I began the practice of "smooth" calling their homes. As we have heard repeatedly, our first contact home should always be a positive one. In some schools, teachers make daily and weekly calls home to let parents know how students are performing, particularly when they are successful. This can become overwhelming at middle school and high school when teachers are responsible for one hundred to two hundred students per day. However "smooth" calls were very beneficial to this end. At the beginning of the year, via curriculum night and email, I would let parents know that they might be receiving what would appear to be a prank call coming from the school at some point during the year. Whenever I gave a summative assessment, I would find the top grades in each of my four science sections. I would then call the number that students had provided after school. Whoever answered the phone, I would simply say, "Smooth," and hang up the phone and laugh as if I had regressed to my middle school self, executing a prank call. This had four tremendous advantages:

1. I could make eight positive home contacts in less than two minutes.

2. It cost me nothing.

3. Students could proudly announce to family and friends that they had been "smooth" called.

4. I got to experience the feeling in the stomach and laughing that comes with prank calling.

Before rejecting this notion as something that your students would think was weird, or something that is beneath the dignity of a teacher, there was remarkable reward for limited work. In fact, I had one mom tell me two years after I had taught her son that he would not let them erase the "smooth" message from their voicemail.

► Answer the questions asked earlier in this section if you have not already:

- How are you unique as a teacher?

- What makes you different than other teachers?

- What works for you when you work with students that might not work for others?

And add this one:

- What is something I could do this week, this month, or this year that would be fun for *me*, with my students?

Let me provide one more example of a student teacher, Rachel Jobe. She was employing the Four Rs to her own practice as she tried to find her footing with classroom management. As her supervisor, I repeatedly asked her to evaluate her techniques and persona with these types of questions:

Are students more engaged?

Are they learning more?

How do we know?

These are powerful questions to ask beginning teachers, but are good questions for accomplished teachers as well. If we are going to collect evidence, then we also need to be ready to admit when something is not working and to shift course midstream. This can happen over the course of a career, year, unit, or lesson. For example, if a lesson is descending into chaos (all teachers have been there), take a moment to stand silently, collect your thoughts, lower your heart rate, and then redirect. After thoughts have been collected and you have a clear direction in mind, then you can speak. In the meantime, silence can be powerful.

During her second week of student teaching, Rachel was having a difficult time getting students' attention. When she used silence, they took that as their cue that it was fine to continue talking. *The Lego Movie* was quite popular at the time, so she decided to use the film to her advantage with her fifth graders. To get their attention, she would say, "Everything is," and the students would respond, with "Awesome"—the amazingly catchy yet banal chorus from the film. This worked very well the first day but then began to backfire the next because students descended into singing the entire song or became increasingly loud. After talking to the students, she modified the strategy by having them respond with frozen silence when she mentioned, the film's evil Krazy Glue, "The KRAGLE." While I am uncertain of how much reflection went into her shift from silence, to the song, to "The KRAGLE," she effectively risked, rejected, and revised.

How Can I Engage Each Student?

This is the question that makes teaching extremely challenging and complex. Simultaneously, this is the question that makes teaching infinitely fascinating. As a beginning teacher, I had the time and energy to spend hours upon hours thinking about this question. Like many other beginning teachers, what I lacked in experience, I tried to make up for with time. My biggest challenge was engaging each student. I considered questioning strategies, collaborative work, new kinds of assessments, and incentive systems. Some strategies worked and some did not, but this was all fodder for reflection. Much of my time was focused on developing games and unique learning experiences for my classroom.

One of the major risks I took was with games and competition in the classroom. The process of developing these games is illustrative of the Four Rs at work. I learned how to effectively run games when I was a student teacher from my cooperating teacher, Jon Gabriele. The genesis of our ideas for games was always precipitated by reflection and predicated on engaging each student. The same was true for competition. Games can be tremendous opportunities to allow students to apply the Four Rs to their own learning if the games are well facilitated. Additionally, games lead to good learning through forced recall and low-stakes quizzing that can strengthen neural pathways. This leads to increased mental acuity, retention, and retrieval (Brown, Roediger, & McDaniel, 2014; Hattie & Yates, 2014; Karpicke, 2012; Willingham, 2009).

One of the few redeeming qualities of video games is that they give students multiple opportunities to fail with little consequence and then the opportunity to learn from that failure. Whether it was the *Tecmo Bowl* or *Super Mario Brothers* in my day, or *Madden* and *Clash of Clans* today, kids can fail and try again after learning from the previous failure. We need to give students those kinds of opportunities in the classroom. There are many games and applications that can make this possible in schools (e.g., *Dreambox, Kahoot, Socrative, Quizlet,* and *Scratch*—we will address how to use these well in subsequent chapters), but like

> Games can be tremendous opportunities to allow students to apply the Four Rs to their own learning if the games are well facilitated.

many others, I worry about even more screen time for students. What are other ways to use games and competition in the classroom?

Competition can be extremely detrimental to motivation. I had to move outside of my egocentric love of competition and sports to create games that were beneficial to all students. If we have had success in school competitions and sports, we have to be extremely careful about assuming that others feel the way we do when considering using competitions in the classroom.

I loved the game "Around the World" in elementary school. The object of the game was to make it around the entire room and back to your seat by beating every other student in class in timed head-to-head battles. The competitors would stand side-by-side next to a desk. The teacher would ask a question—typically a question dependent on rote memorization. The student who answered correctly first moved to the next guess and the loser sat down. If a student successfully beat every member of the class, she would make it back to her seat and would have successfully circumnavigated "the world." Game over. Loved it.

I describe this game in the past tense because I hope that teachers no longer use this horrendous game. I am not referring to the lack of thinking, the pressure, or the constant stream of winners and losers. This was a terrible game for an entirely different reason. The game is extremely demotivating and lacks engagement. Think about the game design. How many students in a class of twenty-five were engaged at one time? That is right—exactly two students or eight percent of the class. That is the most optimistic level of engagement. If the class juggernaut was crushing student after student, it may have been that the class juggernaut was the only student engaged as her opponent may have recognized the futility of trying.

Breaking from my own "apprenticeship of observation" (Lortie, 1975) as a student, I quickly realized that this was a worthless way to play games in the classroom. Over time, I developed and refined ten rules for using games in class. These were developed through many years of reflection, risk, revision, and more than a little rejection. I have used these principles for games for kindergarten to adult participants. In that regard, I believe they are universal.

Ten Rules for Games

1. ***Every* student needs a reason to listen to and answer *every* question *every* time.** This is the single biggest key to using games in the classroom—whether students are using iPads, smart phones, or teachers are pulling Popsicle sticks out of a can—there must be a reason to listen to every question and answer. When I applied this first principle, my games improved dramatically.

(Continued)

(Continued)

2. **Students should love the game.** We do not need a lot of different games. We need to find games that students look forward to playing. This is something that only our students can let us know, so be sure to watch and listen.

3. **The game should manage itself.** Students should want to play the game. If that is the case, losing playing time due to management issues will be a mutual deterrent. Whatever game we are playing, points can be lost and penalties occur when teamwork and sportsmanship are lacking. If we found ourselves having to employ consequences from outside the game, then we know the game is not working.

4. **As the facilitator of the game, you are the unquestioned owner, coach, general manager, commentator, and referee/official.** We cannot allow arguing or hijacking of the game. When students are heavily invested in a game, they will be emotionally engaged. This is good because we know this enhances learning. However, we have to be the definitive voice in the game to ensure fairness, efficiency, and engagement of all. What we say goes. Period.

5. **Attempt to make the game fit the subject whenever possible.** Some of the best games I have seen are math games that apply concepts of probability or arithmetic and are played in partners. If we are doing a review game over vocabulary, math facts, or basic conceptual recall, be sure to design the game accordingly. If we need higher order thinking and recall, be sure to structure the game accordingly. Students cannot give full paragraph answers when playing Jeopardy.

6. **Students should be competing against themselves.** I learned this the hard way. I am fully aware that we do compete against one another in the "real world," but more often we need collaboration. When teams get too far behind and realize they cannot catch up, they give up. This compromises the first principle and is the primary reason for not creating a fixed tournament with winners and losers. To solve this problem, all teams could continue to earn (or lose) points that were cumulative for the quarter. Either the team or the class had to collectively earn a certain number of points so the fact that another team had more points than another team became somewhat irrelevant.

7. **Keep the game close.** While less important when students are competing against themselves, games are much more exciting, and therefore engaging, when they are close. Remember, you are the referee, manager, and commentator—figure out ways to manipulate the game to keep things interesting. One of my favorite methods involves using Popsicle sticks

to randomly call on individuals and teams. You have all of the teams or individuals' names on the sticks in a can. You randomly draw sticks, call the name on the stick, and place the stick back in the can (Do not remove the stick because that team does not need to pay attention until the stick returns to the can.). If you have asked a question that you know a struggling team or individual will know, call that name regardless of what is on the stick. I have been doing it for years—students never know as long as you don't overuse the trick.

8. **Everyone answers.** In order to ensure that everyone is engaged all the time, everyone must be fair game for answering. If they are responding on tablets, whiteboards, or old-fashioned paper, you can have everyone answer and then share. If you are calling on students, be sure every student is a possible option on every question.

9. **Collaboration is key.** When you ask a question, be sure the question is to the entire class. Give students time to discuss the answer with their team—the recall and discussion are where the learning and transition to longer term memory is occurring (Karpicke, 2012). Depending on the complexity of the question, give them appropriate time to answer, which we all know as wait time. Once the answer is given allow a few seconds to pass for other students to consider whether the answer is correct, which is the second form of wait time. Then ask a spokesperson, a role that should rotate, to provide the answer. The team is responsible, but every individual in the classroom should give answers.

10. **You have to look forward to the game yourself.** If you are not enjoying the game, then your students probably are not either. If the game has become tiresome or a management nightmare, it is probably a time for some revision or even rejection—remember, no shame!

Designing and implementing games is a perfect example of the Four Rs at work. If you follow these principles you will be well on your way to designing unique games that are meaningful learning experiences. However, whatever you do, the game will evolve over time as your reflect and revise. This can change from class to class, and year to year. You will know if it is working if you are assessing what students are saying and doing. You will know through feedback from them that you might solicit. You will also know in your finely attuned teacher "gut" after you have done this for a few years. Once you have had some success, you will begin to identify the prospects for future success. The key to good games specifically, and engaged learning in general, is giving our students a chance to struggle, fail, and build on success. As teachers, we also need to struggle, and maybe that struggle will be around developing engaging learning experiences.

▶ How much do you enjoy playing games?

- 1 = "I have and will never like games, even cooperative games."
- 10 = "I love all forms of games."

1	2	3	4	5	6	7	8	9	10

How effective are you at running games?

- 1 = "Bedlam ensues when I run a game."
- 10 = "All students love learning all the time in my games."

1	2	3	4	5	6	7	8	9	10

Think about games you played as a student in school or games you have led as a teacher and answer the following questions:

- Was the game successful?
- What made it successful or unsuccessful?
- Did all students have a reason to be engaged all of the time?
- Did the game manage itself?
- Did *you* have fun?

What is a game you could use, adapt, or develop this year?

When students struggle they have the chance to employ the Four Rs themselves. If we do not provide them with cognitively demanding tasks, there is no reason to reflect, risk, revise or reject. Remember the example of the Japanese student being singled out to struggle on the board as he drew his cube? This was a task that was worthy of the Four Rs.

In my time in classrooms across the U.S., I have never observed this type of public struggle including in my classrooms. That is not to say that this does not occur; it just is not the norm. Most of us would consider this kind of experience humiliating and something that we would avoid for students until the last moments where success was achieved and celebrated. Without the struggle, that celebration is relatively cheap and meaningless. We need to model this kind of struggle for students and celebrate it with them. This is the kind of deep engagement that we need to prioritize in our classrooms. This is how we will get better.

The next four chapters explore overarching practices of good teaching. There are practical applications in each chapter. However, these practices are really a means to apply the mindset and process identified in the first three chapters. This is not meant to be a how-to-teach-in-seven-steps book. As you read, let yourself engage the ideas with an open mind and apply the Four Rs. Aristotle wrote, "It is the mark of an educated mind to be able to entertain a thought without accepting it." If you take Aristotle to heart, then these chapters should be useful for reflection and risk taking of your own. You will start to generate your own ideas that will serve you better than any ideas an author who has never met your students could provide.

Without the struggle, that celebration is relatively cheap and meaningless.

Key Takeaways and Fearless Practices

- Reflect, risk, revise or reject.

- Foster creativity by being willing to be wrong.

- Sometimes rejecting an idea is the best thing to do (e.g., Family Living Q&A and lava lamps)

- Build your personal learning network (PLN). The PLN informs your risks and makes your life easier.

- Your PLN should not add to the amount of time you are working—work smarter not harder.

- Share the results of your risks with your PLN.

- Organize your professional library whether it is physical or digital.

- If you don't apply the Four Rs, you have the potential of teaching your first year for thirty consecutive years.

- Think of your classroom as an Exploratorium.

- Embrace your own quirkiness and that of your students.

- Develop your own version of "smooth" calls.

- Retrieval is essential for learning—play games that engage everyone all the time.

Open-Ended Case Studies

Select one of the teacher case studies below and answer the associated questions.

- You are a twenty-year teaching veteran. Your students are quiet and relatively respectful but are not always as engaged as you would like to see. You do not believe that school should be about entertaining students. You have not had much success with or interest in using games in your classroom. How could you apply the Four Rs to potentially designing a learning game that would increase the engagement of your students? What would be your first steps? What pitfalls would you have to avoid?

- Put yourself in Rachel's position. She is the twenty-one-year-old student teacher who used *The Lego Movie* in her classroom management plan. The class can be a bit rambunctious. She wants to design a game for her class. What challenges might she face that a veteran teacher might not? What steps would she need to take to engage her students? What steps would she need to take to ensure that learning was the central focus of the game? How would the Four Rs assist her in the development of the game?

Reflect

- What is one terrible idea that you tried and rejected? If you are reading this with a group, be sure to share it with others—this might be a great bonding moment and time of commiseration.

- What is one idea that you have developed over time with reflective practice (even if you are a novice, and it is only a short amount of time)?

- How does your PLN make your life as a teacher easier?

- What is the most successful thing you have done to engage all of your students? Be sure to share this with your PLN.

Risk: 3-2-1 Action Steps

3: Identify three people or resources that you can add to your PLN.

Possible steps:

- Observe another teacher in your building and tell her what you learned from the observation.

- Reconnect with a former teacher and professor and ask him for one piece of advice for teaching.

- Find one professional article to read this month.

2: Identify two ideas that you want to develop further and share them with your PLN.

Possible steps:

- Design a new summative assessment for a unit that you have been struggling to know if students are really learning.

- Design a review game for your students.

1: Try one new idea with kids then revise or reject.

Possible steps:

- If you are an experienced teacher, what's a great technique or lesson that you've used for years that is not energizing yourself or students like it once was? How might your revise it to make it better or is it time to reject the idea?

- Play the game you just designed and then get feedback from your students. Revise accordingly.

- Give students your version of a "smooth" call. Reflect, then revise or reject.

Revise or Reject

After taking a risk, determine what to do next. Was it worthy of revision or rejection?

☐ Reject ☐ Revise

Write down a few notes about what worked, what did not, and what you might change.

PART II
Practices

CHAPTER 4

Fill the Classroom

I've had many teachers who taught us soon forgotten things,

But only a few like her who created in me a new thing,
a new attitude, a new hunger.

I suppose that to a large extent I am the unsigned manuscript of
that teacher.

What deathless power lies in the hands of such a person.

from John Steinbeck's *Like Captured Fireflies*

I probably romanticize the classroom. In today's world of virtual, personalized, and online learning, there is debate about the definition of "classroom." Increasingly, we hear about the demise of the "brick and mortar" school and classroom as a relic of the twentieth century. Although I know some of our schools and classrooms look like ancient relics that should be torn down, the notion that classrooms are antiquated makes me sad. I love the smell, feel, and warmth that I associate with vibrant schools—yes even the very "human smell" of middle school classrooms where development has outpaced hygiene.

If I romanticize classrooms, I certainly romanticize the role of the teacher in a learning environment. In my view, this quotation from Steinbeck should be the dream of every teacher. Imagine having been John Steinbeck's high school English teacher. Imagine reading the literature he produced and seeing ripples of the work that you saw beginning in your classroom. Imagine him, immortalizing you with his unique gift—describing himself as "the unsigned manuscript" created by you. You have "deathless power" in your hands. How could there possibly be a more meaningful job?

I think this idealism is useful in that it feeds our optimism about teaching and students. Our purpose as teachers is to pour into students' lives so that they have "a new attitude, a new hunger." Maybe we will never teach a John Steinbeck, but isn't it a lot more inspiring to imagine that this is what our students could become? We are no longer limited to forty-five-minute periods in "brick and mortar" schools. Our engagement with students in our classrooms can extend virtually beyond the time in our physical classrooms, but I am not certain that it can occur entirely online.

My romantic view of teaching as being relational, face-to-face, soul-to-soul interaction does make me wonder if Steinbeck would have written this about an online teacher he had never met. However, we can extend the classroom well beyond the walls where our initial relationship begins. That, in fact, is the job of the teacher today. We must fill the classroom—not in suffocating, authoritarian fashion; instead, we must create space for students to flourish. At minimum, filling the classroom entails Kounin's conceptions of pacing and "withitness" (Kounin, 1970) in the creation of a safe learning environment.

However, I think filling the classroom must be even more than this. A remarkable educator of adults and students, Erik Ellefsen, shared this notion of "filling the classroom" with my preservice teachers several years ago. He described it as an awareness of everything that is going on in the room—or at minimum, the appearance of awareness. We have all had those teachers that really did seem to have eyes in the back of their heads. He went on to describe the way teachers who fill the classroom facilitate and catalyze the work students do. Filling the classroom is not about dominating the space with a big personality. Filling the classroom is about inspiring and supporting outstanding work from students. Filling the classroom is about creating appetite and space for the "unsigned manuscripts" and the "new hunger" and "new attitude."

I mention Erik by name for attribution, but also because of his unique perspective. When he speaks about filling the classroom in order to tap into the "deathless power" of the teacher, he is very aware of his own mortality. Seven years ago, Erik was diagnosed with terminal bone marrow cancer at age 33. He has been through two bone marrow transplants and chemotherapy that nearly killed him. He is in constant pain and discomfort and has a fraction of the energy he had when he was diagnosed. At the time, he was a high school principal completing his dissertation. He was not supposed to live more than five years. To "reduce" his workload, he is now a high school counselor, leads professional development, and connects educators across the country to better serve students. He has never stopped filling his classroom, school, or our profession. Even with a terminal illness and constant physical reminders, he is committed to his students and his colleagues. He once called me from an airport returning from a conference: he said, "I planned it, organized it, and led it. I created a space. I did not get up and speak. I did not moderate, and I was not in front at all. Everything that I wanted to accomplish was accomplished by others."

This is the kind of mindset and perspective that all of us need to bring to our classrooms wherever they might be. This chapter will address three strategies for filling the classroom:

- Create space for growth.
- Engage the entire class.
- Teach students to work hard.

CREATE SPACE FOR GROWTH

The novice mindset has to be all about students. This may seem to contradict what we know about beginning teachers and the challenge of focusing on the needs of their students because they are so self-referential. However, that is why I am referring to the novice mindset and not necessarily novice practices. In order to continue to take risks, reflect, and grow, teachers with the novice mindset have to continually examine what students are saying, doing, and producing. When our focus is on students, our jobs are infinitely interesting and cannot become stale or trite. As we grow in experience, we should become better at creating space for learning.

> I am referring to the novice mindset and not necessarily novice practices. In order to continue to take risks, reflect, and grow, teachers with the novice mindset have to continually examine what students are saying, doing, and producing.

Use Silence

Parker Palmer, writer and teacher, describes this space in *To Know as We are Known.*

> To sit in a class where the teacher stuffs our minds with information, organizes it with finality, insists on having the answers while being utterly uninterested in our views, and forces us into grim competition for grades—to sit in such a class is to experience a lack of space for learning. But to study with a teacher who not only speaks but listens, who not only gives answers but asks questions and welcomes our insights, who provides information and theories that do not close doors but open new ones, who encourages students to help each other learn—to study with such a teacher is to know the power of a learning space. (1993, pp. 70–71)

I have seen this kind of space opened by kindergarten teachers and college professors. This is possible because it is an approach to teaching and learning that transcends practices and techniques. Teachers can create an environment where students question and pursue truth.

Sometimes this can be as simple as using silence. We see this practically speaking in the way we use wait time. Typically, we think of wait time as the time we give students after asking a question. However, we should also consider another type of wait time, wait time two—the time we give students after a student gives an answer.

These two types of wait time are extremely important because we ask so many questions.

Bad News:

- Teachers ask 93 percent of all questions in the classroom and between thirty and one hundred questions per hour (Graesser & Person, 1994).

- Of the questions that teachers ask, 70 percent are at the bottom of Bloom's Taxonomy at the knowledge comprehension levels (Martin, Wood, & Stevens, 1988).

- Over 80 percent of teachers' questions are surface level (Gall, 1984).

- Higher achievers get more wait time and more opportunities to engage in higher order questions (Krueger & Sutton, 2001).

Good News:

- Higher level questions with longer wait time increase achievement (Riley, 1986).

- By extending wait time from one to three seconds:

  o student responses become up to 800 percent longer,
  o speculative and predictive thinking can increase up to 700 percent,
  o low achievers contribute up to 37 percent more,
  o students respond and react more to each other,
  o failure of students to respond decreases,
  o unsolicited but appropriate responses increase.

By simply increasing wait time from one to three seconds for both kinds of wait time, dramatic changes occur in student responses. Student responses become 400–800 percent longer. The number of appropriate but unsolicited responses increases. Failure of students to respond decreases. Low achievers contribute up to 37 percent more. Speculative and predictive thinking can increase as much as 700 percent. Students respond and react more to each other. In essence, by slowing down and adding two seconds of silence, we start to create the classes that we want.

We need each other to do this. Teachers who try to extend wait time from one to three seconds will revert back to one second within four weeks if they are not able to share their experiences with other teachers. This is largely due to the fact that student interactions increase and teachers become uncertain about when to reign in conversation and when to let it continue. With some professional conversation, teachers learn to navigate this increased space (Rowe, 1986).

Why do we give more time to high achievers to answer? Why do they get asked harder questions? I think teachers do this out of good hearts. They do not want to "humiliate" students who struggle. Again, this is because struggle is not viewed as desirable in classrooms in the U.S. We do not want to embarrass students by asking them questions they might not know the answers to and then letting silence settle over the room. Of all the students who need this time, students who struggle are most in need of this extra time. By not giving them time to think and answer we are implying that we do not have high expectations for them. Adding two seconds of wait time will not slow the pace of our classes to the point of boredom for high achievers—we probably do other things that are more responsible for that.

The next time you teach a group of students ask a question and wait three seconds by counting them in your head. If you are like me, that three seconds will seem like a long time.

If you are already good at wait time one, record a class interaction and see how long you wait for wait time two after a student has given an answer. I am terrible at wait time two. I know this because when I force myself to wait for three seconds after a student responds, my students start looking around to see what is wrong. If this wait time were the norm, then students would be building on one another's answers instead of waiting for me to validate the response. Again, we have good intentions for not giving wait time two. We want to encourage the student who has responded, build on it, and bridge to the next concept or question. However, this stops good thinking that might be going on in the classroom and tacitly communicates that teachers are the purveyors of all knowledge.

> This stops good thinking that might be going on in the classroom and tacitly communicates that teachers are the purveyors of all knowledge.

Silence can also work as a means of filling the classroom when we need to get students' attention. Beginning teachers are terrible about attempting to talk over students, pleading/warning the class to be quiet, or just cruising through content unaware of the lack of engagement from their students. Sometimes the best thing we can do when our classes are unaware is square our bodies, put our hands on our hips, and wait silently. For effective teachers, this is often enough of a signal to let students know that expectations are not being met. Additionally, if we find ourselves talking too much and students' attention drifting . . . sometimes a brief pause will get students' attention again.

Palmer summarizes the power of silence for filling and expanding the classroom.

> We need to abandon the notion that "nothing is happening" when it is silent, to see how much new clarity a silence often brings . . . In most places where people meet, silence is a threatening experience. It makes us self-conscious and awkward; it feels like some kind of failure . . . But once the silence is established with a group, once we learn that we make progress being quiet, then silence becomes a potent space for learning. (1993, pp. 80–81)

Silence then is a powerful tool for creating a "potent space for learning" but it may not feel that way at first and certainly will not work on its own. I have seen many teachers stand at the front of the class, silently waiting for the class to calm down, and the class sees this as an opportunity to continue in its frivolity. We need more ways to fill the classroom.

Fearless Reflection

▶ How would you rate your students' willingness to share in class?

- 1 = "When I ask a question I hear crickets."
- 10 = "100 percent of my students want to share all of the time."

1	2	3	4	5	6	7	8	9	10

Now think about the quality of their thinking—think about the level of academic vocabulary, syntax, and discourse. How would you rate the quality of what they share?

- 1 = "My students are clueless."
- 10 = "All of my students contribute to thoughtful, creative discourse."

1	2	3	4	5	6	7	8	9	10

How could wait time one help with this? How would you rate yourself on using wait time one?

- 1 = "My students are lucky if I ask a question."
- 10 = "I am a master—three seconds or more every time."

1	2	3	4	5	6	7	8	9	10

How would you rate yourself on using wait time two?

- 1 = "My students are lucky if I wait to hear the first answer."
- 10 = "I am a master—three seconds or more every time."

1	2	3	4	5	6	7	8	9	10

Expand the Walls of the Classroom

Learning has never been confined to the walls of the classroom. That is truer now than ever with smart phones putting the world at students' fingertips. Good teachers have never been afraid of this expansion of the classroom. In fact, I would argue that this is the most exciting time in the history of civilization to be teachers, we just need to help students direct and harness the learning that can go beyond the classroom and teach them to assess and reflect upon what, why, and how they are learning.

This is more than flipping the classroom so that lectures are viewed at home and work is done in the classroom. Flipping the classroom is something that good English language arts teachers and science teachers have been doing for years. The preparation done at home might include reading, some initial thinking, or some note taking, but the real work takes place in the labs and workshops that occur in class. This is a great model for learning and helping students understand how they are progressing so that they can seek appropriate supports. However, can you imagine how that would work if high school students were expected to go home at night and watch eight fifteen-minute lectures? Expanding the walls of the classroom is not something that can be standardized, but there are several elements that can work for all teachers.

> Expanding the walls of the classroom is not something that can be standardized, but there are several elements that can work for all teachers.

One of those elements is the move away from behavioral objectives toward learning goals and targets (Chappuis, Stiggins, Chappuis, & Arter, 2006; Marzano, Pickering, & Heflebower, 2011; Moss & Burhart, 2012). The major shift really has to do with assessment. With good objectives, teachers are able to observe student progress toward a goal that they have in mind. The learning target shifts the responsibility of assessment from just teachers to teachers and students.

> The learning target shifts the responsibility of assessment from just teachers to teachers and students.

Both parties are responsible for reflecting on progress toward an agreed upon target. In most conceptions of the learning target, the goal is meant to be set based on what students can achieve in one lesson. This aids assessment for novice teachers and self-assessment and self-efficacy for students. Now, instead of seeing lesson plans with five to six objectives for one lesson, we only select one learning target—a huge win for clarity and concision (See Fearless Reflection Box).

If teachers use big, broad, abstract essential questions (Wiggins & McTighe, 2005) to drive units, then they can use learning targets to drive the days that will make up those units. If students are aware of what those learning targets are, and are regularly asked to reflect on their progress toward them, their learning can occur anywhere within those parameters. In essence, students will be applying the Four Rs to their own learning. One of the primary purposes of using the Four Rs as teachers is to model this for students. Being transparent with our reflection, risking, revising, and rejection will communicate the power of learning from success and failure. But modeling is not enough. We need to give them the tools and opportunities to do this with their own learning.

▶ Below is a comparison of learning targets and behavioral objectives with examples. Which do you find to be more helpful?

Learning Targets	Behavior Objectives
• Driven by essential questions	• Driven by essential questions
• Teacher and student understand	• Teacher understands
• Teacher and student assess progress	• Teacher assesses progress
• Lesson-sized goal	• Could be many for one lesson
• Formative assessment—throughout and at the end of the lesson	• Possible formative or summative assessment
• Example: I will identify three minerals based on a distinctive physical property.	• Example: Students will be able to classify rocks and minerals according to their physical properties such as: color, luster, hardness, streak, texture, and chemical properties.

ENGAGE THE ENTIRE CLASS

Think back to the embarrassing teaching that comprised the opening vignette of this book. I had approximately 12 percent of my class engaged in my lesson. Far from creating space for deeper student-owned learning, I had not even engaged students at a basic level. In many great classrooms that I get to observe, I see master teachers with students engaged in all different types of learning while they work with small groups or float around the room asking well-timed questions to prompt deeper learning. I have seen master teachers do this from kindergarten through college. This is an ideal way to engage all students, in that students are engaged in work that they own and is relevant to them.

However, great teachers can also make whole class instruction work extremely well for students. This next section will explore some ways to do this. Be sure to approach this from the learning stance of a novice, and as always be sure to apply the Four Rs.

Effectively Use Technology

One of the few areas where novice teachers are expected to be more adept than veteran teachers is in the use of technology. While most millennials are comfortable with digital media and approach technology without fear, that does not mean they know how to use it effectively for instruction. They may be less likely to create banal PowerPoints that will bullet point students into bored submission, but they may not apply technology effectively. Merriam-Webster's online dictionary defines technology as "a manner of accomplishing a task especially using technical processes, methods, or knowledge." If this is the definition of technology, then there are many ways to use processes, methods, or knowledge to accomplish learning targets. Many of these tools are outstanding for basic formative assessment as everyone can respond. Those responses can be recorded anonymously or by name. Best of all for cash-strapped teachers, all of these are free.

> Plickers – This is a class response system where students hold Quick Response (QR) codes that have been assigned to them. They can rotate them four ways which gives them the opportunity to respond "A, B, C, or D." The teacher can then scan the entire class with her smartphone through the Plickers app, and student responses show up immediately on her phone. Feedback is immediate and scores are stored online. Two words of warning: do not laminate the QR codes because the glare makes them difficult for the phone to read, and be sure that students' fingers do not cover any part of the QR code or the phone cannot read it. Plickers are great for students who do not have their own devices and is superior to individual whiteboards where students can easily look at answers of other students or be self-conscious of their own.

> Kahoot – This is my new favorite. With mesmerizing "lobby music," fun yet stress-inducing countdown tones, and the opportunity for anyone with an online device, this is perfect for children and adults. Respondents log in using a game specific code on the screen and create a screen name. For those students who decide to create a less than appropriate screen name, wily Kahoot renames them. Depending on students' technological acuity age, logging in can take between fifteen seconds and three minutes. Similar to most other response systems, there are four answer options. There can be more than one correct answer. Respondents earn large quantities of points based on the speed with which they accurately answer questions. After each question the standings appear on the board. I have had groups of forty teachers yelling, cheering, and aggressively competing to move up the Kahoot scoreboard. Engagement is always high.

> Socrative – This is another tool that allows for real time questioning and immediate visualization of student understanding. Socrative does require students to have tablets, laptops, or smartphones. This is ideal for quick formative assessment and survey activities that foster discussion. Socrative also provides reports on student responses.

> Nearpod – I first saw this used in a fifth-grade classroom with a cart full of laptops. Students were extremely engaged once they were able to log in which took some students several minutes due to issues with the school's Wi-Fi. After they were on, students were extremely engaged and

did not earn points as a team unless every member of the team answered correctly—an adaptation made by the teacher. This certainly increased the collaborative nature of the engagement. The application is similar to Socrative in that it tracks responses and provides reports on student performance.

Jeopardy – I am certain that most students have never seen the Alex Trebek television-version of Jeopardy; however, they are familiar with this game from school. Here are a couple of benefits and a twist. Jeopardy allows large groups of students to confer, discuss, and answer questions. There are free hyperlinked PowerPoint slide templates available online. Teachers can keep the different games from unit to unit and year to year and modify as needed. The twist that my seventh graders loved was our "Potpourri" category as the last column. This classic Jeopardy category included answers that were all about them (e.g., "The basketball player who scored fourteen points in last night's game," or "Most likely to try to delay class by asking teachers questions to elicit a story."). Yes, this is a waste of five academic questions, but the excitement this generated due to the beautiful narcissism of middle school students was well worth the four minutes of class time.

Quizlet – On a smartphone, tablet, or computer, students can create their own Quizlet account and use flashcards, tests, or study games that teachers and students all over the world have developed. Students and teachers can track progress, create their own study sets, and compete against other students. The Quizlet site claims that more people study on Quizlet every day than on any other educational software.

Scratch – Developed by MIT, this online tool allows students to learn how to write code. Tammie Schrader, an award-winning middle school science teacher in Washington, has her students write code through Scratch to explain key scientific concepts. In a classic example of the novice mindset, she said, "I was 10 minutes ahead of them before they logged in. Now they are long gone." Students don't just write code for the sake of writing code; they write the code to better understand and articulate key science concepts.

Fearless Reflection

▶ How effective are you at using technology to increase student engagement?

- 1 = "These new slates to write on with chalk are amazing."

- 10 = "I have written Individualized Education Plans for each student and they are constantly engaged through seamless technology integration."

| 1 | 2 | 3 | 4 | 5 | 6 | 7 | 8 | 9 | 10 |

How would your students rate you?

1	2	3	4	5	6	7	8	9	10

What could you do to improve your use of technology or help others improve?

I have found these technology tools to be effective. Certainly there are many other tools—be sure to share them. Maybe start by sharing an attempt at incorporating technology that backfired (e.g., a terribly crafted PowerPoint, terrible game, or problematic website). Then, share one technology tool you have used (or will use) that increases all students' engagement in your classes with a colleague, in a professional learning community (PLC), or with your personal learning network (PLN).

Signal Not to Be Called On

Teachers have a Pavlovian response to hand raising. When we see a hand go up, we want to call on that student. Many of us have learned to fight that urge to increase wait time or include other students, but we still struggle with what to do with students who do not raise their hands.

Many elementary teachers I know were relatively good students. They liked school. They played "school." They made the decision to spend a career in a school. Certainly there are many exceptions to this, and as we move into middle school and high school teachers, we find a wide array of former student types. I bring this up because like everyone, teachers are egocentric. For the former student who wanted to please her teacher, being called on to answer a question she did not know was humiliating. The thought of doing that to a student in her own classroom is out of the question. However, what about those students who have learned that they never actually have to answer a question or engage in a discussion?

In my seventh grade science classes, I implemented a policy that required students to signal me not to be called on. The signal was making eye contact with me and giving me a smile. Anything else (e.g., looking out the window, making eye contact with a friend, scratching a head) was a signal to be called on. This put the onus on students who did not want to be called on to engage with me while reducing anxiety for students who were anxious about being called on without raising their hands—they were already giving me eye contact.

> I implemented a policy that required students to signal me not to be called on.

In an era of learning walks, instructional rounds, and unannounced observations, this method has another interesting advantage. When my principal would enter the room during any type of whole class instruction she would see me asking numerous higher order questions. Sometimes I overestimated what students would know or be willing to share in these interactions. On two occasions, she complimented my classes for being particularly attentive and engaged because all of them were making eye contact and smiling at me when I was asking questions. When she left the room, after a slight delay to ensure that she was out of earshot, my students erupted in laughter because they knew the reason they looked so engaged was that none of them knew the answers to my overzealous questions.

Use Proximity and Nonverbal Cues

Most of the effective teachers I have observed rarely have to verbally redirect students. With a look, motion, or proximity, they are able to communicate expectations and refocus students' attention. The fewer words we can use to direct behavior, the more we can focus students on the work at hand. These nonverbal cues are the beginning of what Lemov (2010, 2015) calls the "least invasive form of intervention."

Movement around the room is always essential. One issue with document cameras and presentation hardware is that it can cause teachers to be rooted to one spot in the classroom. As teachers, we should always be circulating, even during whole class interactions and particularly if students are using technology devices. While talking to the entire class or facilitating collaborative work, simply positioning ourselves near students who are off-task can sometimes be enough. Sometimes a tap of a teacher's finger on a desk can bring a student out of a daydream. In other instances, it may be the teacher's "stink eye"—that look that communicates equal parts disappointment, disapproval, and redirection. We have all seen this from a teacher or parent and know that some stink eyes are more effective than others. I have actually assigned the development of the stink eye to some of my more unassuming preservice teachers. They have to spend time in front of a mirror perfecting a no-nonsense look. For some kind souls, this can take weeks to develop without breaking into a counterproductive smile.

All of these teacher moves can be useful, but we can be even more thoughtful about how we use proximity. For example, when we are facilitating a whole class discussion, where we position ourselves for that discussion matters. We know we should be circulating around the room as students seamlessly transition between partner, small group, and whole group interaction. If we begin to engage an individual or small group in discussion, we have to be sure to position ourselves so we can see the most students possible (See Figure 4.1). Novice teachers tend to lack awareness of the entire class when they begin to engage with a small group of students. Some will turn their backs on the rest of the class—remember back to my initial fourth-grade teaching video.

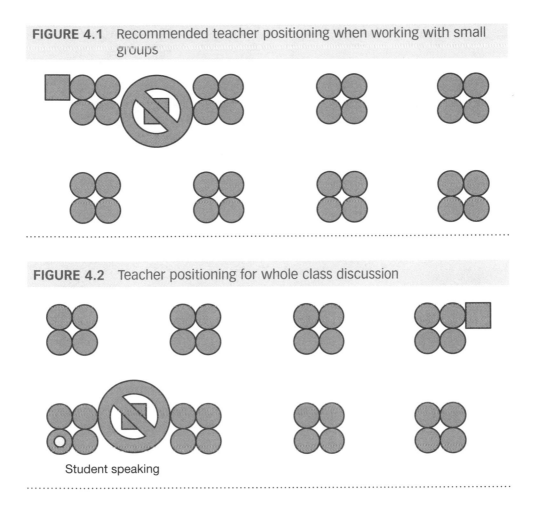

FIGURE 4.1 Recommended teacher positioning when working with small groups

FIGURE 4.2 Teacher positioning for whole class discussion

Student speaking

Another useful, but counterintuitive idea that I have discovered from leading class discussions with six-year-olds to adults, is that I need to move away from the speaker as far as I can when she is talking. This is counterintuitive because we have a natural tendency to want to move toward a speaker to communicate immediacy and a desire to hear what she has to say. However, in a discussion setting, we want to include the entire class in the conversation (See Figure 4.2). This has two benefits. First, the entire class has a sense that they are part of the interaction. Second, this requires the student to project her answer for all to hear. When we move farther away, we ensure that if we can hear the student, then everyone else in the class can hear the student. If we move closer, it becomes awkward for the student to project the answer for a student who is thirty feet away if the person who has asked the question is three feet away.

> I need to move away from the speaker as far as I can when she is talking.

Create a Façade of Omnipresence

If our classrooms are going to prioritize independent and collaborative work, then many times it will seem as if a teacher needs to be in six places at the same time. While this is not possible, I have observed many teachers where this seems to be the case. I have seen this in elementary and college classrooms. There will be five groups of students in the first-grade class all doing different components of a reading program. The teacher is sitting at a kidney table with five students in front of her with all of her other students in view. The groups are all working well. The teacher seems completely focused on the individuals in her group, but suddenly she says in a firm voice, "Tony, open your book back up and continue reading." A boy on the other side of the room, whom you had not noticed, immediately opens his book and begins reading.

In an eleventh-grade classroom, it might be a chemistry teacher moving from lab station to lab station focusing on the work of various lab partners. He observes two students more engaged in some tremendously important Instagram post than their lab work. Without even making eye contact, he redirects them back to their work, by walking over to them and tapping their lab reports. The students appear to be surprised, thinking that their temporary lack of engagement had gone unnoticed under the lab table.

This type of withitness (Kounin, 1970) is not the practice of the typical novice. The more experience and reflection a teacher logs, the more sensitive she becomes to student learning and engagement. This is one of the amazing aspects of the novice mindset—teaching can become increasingly interesting over the course of our careers. As we become more aware of everything occurring in our classrooms, and have a better sense of how our students think and learn, our work becomes more interesting. The content requires less of our mental energy, which liberates us to focus on our students and how they are engaging their own learning. Having taught some labs sixteen times in four years, if the content had been the focus for me, I would have started to experience burnout. But, as I became more aware of my seventh grade students' ever-changing minds and personalities driven by hormonal relational chaos, my science classroom was infinitely fascinating. Being aware of all of your students at all times is daunting, but the benefits go far beyond classroom management. While the ultimate goal is omnipresence in the classroom, for most of us mortals, we get as close as possible and allow a façade to suffice for the difference between reality and the ideal.

Fearless Reflection

▶ How omnipresent are you in your classroom?

- 1 = "I didn't know there were other human beings in my classroom."

- 2 = "I know the breathing rate of all my students at any given time."

| 1 | 2 | 3 | 4 | 5 | 6 | 7 | 8 | 9 | 10 |

Think of a teacher you know as a colleague or you knew as a student who seemed omnipresent.

- What does he or she do that makes this seem to be the case?

- What might you try with your own students to impress upon them that you are aware of everything occurring in the classroom? Is this even possible? If so, how?

TEACH STUDENTS TO WORK HARD

So many well-meaning teachers completely hamstring their students by not clearly defining the work of students and the teacher and then providing supports for both parties to successfully do their jobs. Tom Thibodeau, the former head coach of the Chicago Bulls, was a notorious hard worker and extremely demanding coach. During games (and I am certain in practices as well), he could be heard yelling three simple words that he believed should be the only motivation a player needed. In his deep, gravelly voice, he would growl, "Do your job."

In essence this is what we need to do for and with students—with support and direction for how to do that job. We must define their work and hold them accountable for that work. We must define our work and hold ourselves accountable. Many well-intentioned teachers do not do this. Whether it is out of a desire to see projects turn out well, save students from humiliation, or a lack of understanding of the benefits of struggle, many teachers do the students' work for them. Robyn Jackson's book, *Never Work Harder Than Your Students* (2009), identifies how good intentions of teachers can lead to learned helplessness of students. Students realize that the teacher will do the work for them if they just wait long enough. This is not the way to fill the classroom. If we are going to make room for students to work, then they need to be doing challenging, relevant work that is worthy of their time.

> If we are going to make room for students to work, then they need to be doing challenging, relevant work that is worthy of their time.

How many of us knew teachers who would give the answers to tests if we asked questions during the exam the right way? How many teachers do we know who look at the name at the top of the paper and grade leniently due to perceived strengths or weaknesses of the student on prior performance? How many of us have removed projects from our curriculum because students or parents have complained that they are too much work or in order to "cover" more standards? If students are unmotivated to work hard, or we are perpetuating a culture of compliance, then we are failing to fill the classroom.

Set Parameters for Work Based on Your Roles

Teachers set the parameters for the learning environment. We provide materials, support and direction, but students work. For example, Jackson (2009) asserts that teachers should not be rewarding *students* for good work; instead, teachers should celebrate the good *work* that students are doing. This subtle shift in emphasis keeps the focus on the work and not the teacher.

In addition to celebrating good work, teachers have to help students clearly define that work. Clear learning targets, rubrics, student examples, formative assessments, and self-assessments all help in the definition of the work in that expectations are operationalized. Moreover, when we provide these supports, students have an opportunity to reflect back to us what we think we have communicated. The work that is expected should never be a mystery. However, there should be latitude wherever possible for students to develop their own voices and exert autonomy.

This balance between clarity of the expected work and student autonomy can be challenging, but makes parameters for the work absolutely essential. As students, we have likely all been frustrated by teachers or professors who give extremely open-ended assignments which we work hard on, only to receive a less than optimal grade when it turns out that we did not meet the opaque standards known only to the mind of the instructor. Again, this can lead to learned helplessness for students if they do not feel that their work will impact the outcome. Ironically, the best way to successfully give students choice and autonomy that will lead to productive learning is to provide guidelines that make the goals of the work explicit and understandable.

Clear learning targets, student samples, and rubrics can do a great deal to support hard work. When those are coupled with strong formative assessment that prioritizes growth, student learning and the quality of student work flourish. For every major assignment in my preservice teaching classes, students turn in a draft of their best work at least three weeks before the final draft is due. Then I provide them with written and oral feedback and set aside one hour and fifty minute blocks of class time to meet with individual students while they meet in groups to do the work of refining their assignments. The workload for me at the formative checkpoint is significant, but when the final summative assessment is due, my work is largely done. Ultimately this serves two purposes: assessment becomes about growth and I can assure anyone that students in our program are capable of meeting and exceeding the outcomes we set forth for our program. These two assertions are not based on my conjecture, but the evidence that my students' work provides. Then, instead of checking a box for licensure or students feeling as if they are being given a grade, we can celebrate the work that they have done.

Fearless Reflection

▶ Some teachers can become very focused on projects students will produce in their classes. In the past, this may have been a poster project, sugar cube pyramid, or diorama. Today, maybe it is a Prezi, webpage, or blog. We want them to look a certain way or we don't want to share the work of every student— maybe just a few exemplars. To accomplish this, we (or even worse, hope that parents might) may begin to take back some of the work that should belong to students.

- What problems could this cause?

- What can we do to ensure that we set clear parameters that will increase the likelihood that each student will work to his/her capacity?

- How might we modify or create an assignment that would prioritize quality student work?

Every Minute Matters

I love teachers who are jealous of time. If they have students for a fifty-two-minute period, they want every one of those fifty-two minutes and might try to steal minute fifty-three from a passing period. This desire to use every minute sends a message to students about the importance we place on learning and hard work in our classrooms.

Learning targets are essential to communicating that every minute matters. How much can students learn in a fifty-two-minute period? Not only that, but how can they demonstrate that learning? This is very difficult to determine as a beginning teacher with students that you might not know very well, but it is a useful discipline. If this learning is what is driving our instruction and we are setting challenging learning targets then we will not have any time to waste.

Bell work, work that students do immediately when they get to their desks, communicates the urgency of our work. This can take various forms depending on grade level and subject area, but the work should be meaningful and directly related to the learning target. The work can be collaborative or individual, but it should challenge students to mentally engage the subject at hand.

After the bell work, we should express clear expectations for what will follow. Knowing what to do when bell work is completed eliminates downtime that could derail the remainder of the lesson. If there is time when some students finish work early, that "sponge time" should be structured where students know exactly what options they have for extending their learning. This can be as simple as always having a book to read and as complex as subject-specific enrichment.

According to Steinbeck, students are our "unsigned manuscripts." If that is the case then we want them to take the knowledge, skills, and habits of mind that they have cultivated in our classrooms to the work they will do in the future. As teachers, we want students to be motivated to work hard, but more importantly, we want them to be motivated by hard work. In the next chapter, we will explore how to tap into this motivation strategically.

Key Takeaways and Fearless Practices

- Students are our "unsigned manuscripts."
- Fill the classroom by expanding walls, not suffocating those inside.
- Use silence to create space.
- Increase wait time from one to three seconds.
- Use wait time two.
- Challenge all students with difficult questions and give them time to think.
- Use learning targets so that you and your students can track progress toward goals.
- Use big, broad, abstract essential questions.
- Do not use technology for the sake of using technology. Use technology to enhance and facilitate learning.
- Have students give you signals not to call on them.
- Move to the other side of the room when you call on a student.
- Develop your "stink eye."
- Position yourself so you can see your entire class all the time.
- Create a façade of omnipresence.
- Teach students to work hard by giving respectful tasks where your role and their role are clear.
- Emphasize that every minute of class time matters by facilitating meaningful work.

Open-Ended Case Studies

Select one of the teacher case studies and answer the associated questions.

- You are a first-year teacher. You were hired to teach at an urban elementary school two weeks prior to the start of the school year. You have been spending sixteen hours a day in your room trying to organize what materials the previous teacher left behind and the district has provided. You live in another neighborhood in the city and have not had time to get to know the culture of the school or community. What would be three things that you would do in the first week to create space, engage each student, and teach students to work hard?
- Anna Baker is a special education teacher at a charter school in Denver. She taught for three years in a charter school in Chicago, took a year off, and then returned to teaching last year. Her school starts each day with a kick-off meeting for teachers at 7:05 AM and dismissal is between 4:00–15. She loves the environment of her new school and the collaborative nature of the faculty. She does not have

her own classroom but has done home visits, plans with other teachers, and pushes into their classrooms to support students. Not having her own classroom, how can Anna create space, engage students, and teach students to work hard?

Reflect

- What is one way you have been successful in creating space for students? How could you create even more space? What concerns you about creating space for students?

- What is one way you have extended the walls of your classroom? How successful was this?

- When are students most engaged in your class? How could you increase the amount of time where students are highly engaged?

- How do you effectively communicate that every minute matters in your class?

- How can you empower students to do the work that belongs to them? As a teacher, how can you step back and support to give students the freedom to lead?

Risk: 3-2-1 Action Steps

3: Identify three ways you can create space for students.

Possible steps:

- Increase wait time one and two to three seconds. Be sure to process what happens in your class with a colleague.

- Give students at least three options for the next assignment that you will assess.

2: Try two new ideas from your PLN for engaging students.

Possible steps:

- Try letting students signal you to not be called on. Give it at least a week.

- Try a new game or technology application.

1: Implement one idea that will make each student work harder in your class.

Possible step:

- Give students an assignment with clear expectations. Have students submit the assignment significantly early. Give them formative feedback that will push all students to work harder.

Revise or Reject

After taking a risk, determine what to do next. Was it worthy of revision or rejection?

☐ Reject   ☐ Revise

Write down a few notes about what worked, what did not, and what you might change.

CHAPTER 5

Motivate Pragmatically

"Those three things—autonomy, complexity, and a connection between effort and reward—are, most people will agree, the three qualities that work has to have if it is to be satisfying."

Malcolm Gladwell in *Outliers: The Story of Success*

Work satisfaction is dependent on autonomy, complexity, and connection between effort and reward. We do not often think about this for students, but why wouldn't this apply to them as well as us? Shouldn't school be satisfying for them as well? Isn't it possible for teachers to build experiences that increase autonomy, complexity, and a connection between effort and reward?

These seem like fairly straightforward questions, with straightforward answers. Yes, this should apply to students. Yes, school should be satisfying for teachers *and* students. Yes, it is possible to create these conditions. However, in a recent survey, only 40 percent of teachers and administrators reported that students at their schools are highly motivated. Yet 94 percent of respondents feel they are good at engaging and motivating their students (Education Week Research Center, 2014).

Which all begs the questions: Why isn't school more satisfying for students? Why aren't students more motivated?

To answer those two questions, we will explore what it means to pragmatically motivate students. In the last chapter, we started to examine intrinsic motivation through doing good work and emphasizing growth. For some veteran teachers, this may seem a bit naïve. They may not have met many intrinsically motivated high school math students who learn geometry simply for the satisfaction of understanding it. In my experience, that is a fair observation. Beginning teachers might believe that this kind of intrinsic motivation exists. This can be good if the teacher raises expectations or has additional passion and energy for the subject due to this naiveté, but this expectation of intrinsically motivated students can also be problematic.

For example, student teachers become disillusioned when they enter classrooms where students are not intrinsically motivated to learn. Below is an anonymous, archetypal example with illustrative comments that I hear from student teachers. We'll call the student teacher Sarah.

First week of student teaching:

Sarah: "I love my students. They are so fun."

Me: "What have you noticed about them?"

Sarah: "Well they are a really talkative group, and I don't want to be critical [Sure sign that criticism is coming], but they don't seem very motivated. My cooperating teacher is great, but he does not seem to be able to intrinsically motivate them [Note the problematic nature of this assumption]."

Second week of student teaching:

Me: "How was your week?"

Sarah: "I got to teach second period. My students are still great, but they don't listen to me the way they do my cooperating teacher. My lesson was great, but they really did not seem that motivated. This is a really tough class. Some of the other classes are easier to motivate."

Fifth week of student teaching:

Me: "How much are you teaching now?"

Sarah: "I have all six periods. Teaching is hard—all my students have tough home lives, but I love my kids. I am really tired and am having a hard time keeping students engaged and motivated. The last period of the day is really hard—they are checked out. I am not sure what to do—they just don't seem to care, and I really want them to love my subject. I told myself I would never use rewards, but I may have to."

Twelfth week of student teaching:

Sarah: "I am not sure I can be a teacher. My students just don't care about my subject, and I just can't seem to make them care about school."

Fearless Reflection

Who does Sarah blame first for the lack of "intrinsic motivation"?

Who does Sarah blame at week two?

Who does Sarah blame at week five?

Who does Sarah blame at week twelve?

Where are there fallacies in Sarah's thinking?

Notice that I did not need to prompt Sarah with a question on the first week or the twelfth week. The emotion she was feeling caused her to share without prompting. At first, Sarah blamed the cooperating teacher for not being able to motivate students—this is very typical for beginning teachers, as it can be easy to judge out of ignorance. Anyone can sit at the back of a classroom and observe someone else and find ways to be critical. Then she blamed a particular class. Next, she blamed the home lives of "all" of her students in general and the end of the day for one class in particular. Finally, she blamed herself and her lack of agency to do anything about student motivation. There are many fallacies in her thinking that will be explored in the remainder of the chapter.

The most common fallacy that I hear when teachers begin to talk in defeated ways about intrinsic motivation is that the teacher should be able to "intrinsically" motivate students.

In order to effectively engage students, students must be motivated to learn. However, the most common fallacy that I hear when teachers begin to talk in defeated ways about intrinsic motivation is that the teacher should be able to "intrinsically" motivate students. Intrinsic means, "occurring as a natural part of something." Based on this definition, no one can "intrinsically" motivate you. Teachers must come to this realization. Intrinsic motivation must come from within. Therefore, as teachers, the most we can hope for is to help students tap into that inner drive. To do that, we may need to use some good extrinsic motivation—we must become pragmatic motivators in order to make students' work satisfying and meaningful.

STOP SETTING OURSELVES UP FOR FAILURE

Intrinsic motivation is useful for long-term growth but must come from within the student. If we believe we can "give" students this type of motivation, then we are setting ourselves up for failure. This is particularly problematic for beginning teachers because they are the most prone to this type of misguided idealism. When they cannot do this, they believe they have failed. What is a reasonable approach to motivation that is both realistic and sustainable? What motivation can teachers provide that will be most likely to develop intrinsic motivation in the most students?

Alfie Kohn (1994) argues that extrinsic rewards diminish intrinsic motivation. I would agree that stickers, stars, general praise, and most awards do little to develop intrinsic motivation. Imagine an elementary teacher who is conditioning desired behavior by giving Jolly Ranchers for every desirable behavior. The students are being treated in a manner reminiscent of Pavlov's dogs. What happens when that positive reinforcement of the behavior is taken away? The motivation for the behavior goes away—motivation that may have been there in the first place.

We see this happen all of the time as teachers and parents when we misapply rewards. Take for example, Ben, a twelve-year-old boy, who really wants to learn how to mow the grass because it involves machinery and an adult tool. He happily mows the lawn, and then a parent decides he should give Ben ten dollars as a token of appreciation for mowing the grass. The next time Ben mows the grass, he is going to expect the ten dollars. If the money does not appear, his motivation to mow will likely diminish. Granted, over time, the "reward" of using machinery and an adult tool would have diminished, but the financial reward reduced the work to a transaction. The student then deems that the work is not worthy of time without the associated reward. This is the type of extrinsic motivation that Kohn warns against.

Bearing in mind this stipulation, there are rewards that are extrinsic motivators that could ultimately lead to intrinsic motivation. Sometimes those rewards are necessary for a time and can then be diminished or reduced. Think about how a parent might teach a child to love reading. A child snuggles up next to a parent to read a book of his or her choosing. For years, the parent reads books aloud in this manner. The child may not be intrinsically drawn to reading. For both the parent and the child, the reward is the closeness that comes from this experience and maybe the great illustrations. As the child develops, the parent transitions the reading responsibility to the child. Maybe the parent goes over basic phonics rules or how to sound out words. The child might struggle, so the parent offers some type of reward for reading for a period of time—maybe screen time or a particular privilege. Until the child reaches a certain level of proficiency, reading in itself is not enjoyable. When children can read fluently, then they have the chance to tap into an intrinsic desire to learn about the world or the human experience through books.

The same is true of motivation for teachers. Teachers are well known for claiming that they "do not teach for the money." This is true in some respects because there are far stronger motivations for teaching than money (Deci & Flaste, 1995; Pink, 2009; Rodriguez & Fitzpatrick, 2014). However, money does matter to teachers. In researching districts across the country who are implementing changes to evaluations, supports, and compensation for teachers, I have found that money does matter to teachers particularly when new initiatives are being introduced (Eckert, 2010, 2013). Teachers tell me that additional compensation is often needed at the onset of more rigorous efforts to improve student outcomes if they are being asked to take on additional work. As these initiatives progress, many teachers cited the additional support and increased collaboration that resulted in better teaching and learning as the most valuable part of their work. While still valued, the additional compensation became less important as the more rewarding work took hold.

These two examples demonstrate the need to use extrinsic motivation strategically. As teachers, we do not want to get through the year only to see the gains we realized with students lost in subsequent years because we were only good at manipulating them to perform with shortsighted extrinsic rewards. Thoughtful use

> We do not want to get through the year only to see the gains we realized with students lost in subsequent years because we were only good at manipulating them to perform with shortsighted extrinsic rewards.

of extrinsic motivation can lead to higher levels of intrinsic motivation or at least better forms of motivation that delay gratification.

Fearless Reflection

▶ How good are you at motivating your students?

- 1 = "I bore my students into submission."
- 10 = "I am the Tony Robbins of teaching—I can get my students to do anything."

1   2   3   4   5   6   7   8   9   10

- Have you ever felt like a failure due to lack of student motivation? If so, how did you overcome it? If you have not overcome it, what could you try?

- Have you ever used extrinsic rewards? If so, how?

- If you have not, what motivates your students?

- What are some other examples where students might be extrinsically motivated to a good end?

PRAGMATIC MOTIVATION

There are four ways that we will briefly explore to pragmatically motivate students:

- Make learning relevant
- Give students choices
- Establish and uphold consequences
- Cultivate a future-orientation

Make Learning Relevant

Educators agree that one of the best ways to motivate students and catch glimpses of what might be intrinsic motivation is to make our classes relevant

(Education Week Research Center, 2014). We know that we can differentiate through process—how students learn; product—what they produce; content—what they learn; and environment—how the learning environment and materials are organized (Tomlinson & Moon, 2013). These are the primary areas where we can make learning relevant for students. This can occur through the way students work together, the outcome of the work, or the content that is the focus of the work. With my middle school students, the more the work could be about them, the more engaged they were. In reading in particular, researchers have found that engagement based on perceived relevance and the nature of the content directly affects the reading ability of students (Guthrie, 2008) and particular groups of readers respond differently to particular content (Tatum, 2006). Giving them a voice in decision-making and improvement-related processes can lead to school improvement (Quaglia & Corso, 2014).

In a conversation with one parent of a fifth-grade girl in Graham's (the first-year teacher from the first chapter) class, a mother illustrated the power a teacher can have on motivating a student. I asked how her daughter had done in his class this year. She said, "She is a reader now. I have always struggled to get her to read. This year, she was always reading because Graham would read books with her. He would take the same book home at night and they would discuss it the next day as they read."

Before trying to come up with clever ways to manipulate and motivate students, we need to use our expertise as teachers to connect curriculum to what we know about our students. This could be through the reading materials we select, writing prompts, particular historical events, or types of artistic work. As teachers, we know our classroom contexts better than anyone and must take advantage of that knowledge to engage our students. If we use the novice mindset and are continually applying the Four Rs, then we will continually find ways to engage students through relevance.

> Before trying to come up with clever ways to manipulate and motivate students, we need to use our expertise as teachers to connect curriculum to what we know about our students.

Making Learning Relevant: Tammie Schrader

"I spoke at the White House on gaming and programming in the classroom, and I am not a gamer or a programmer."

These are the humble words of a true perpetual novice, Tammie Schrader. We have to back up twenty-five years to understand how she got to the point that she was speaking at the White House. Tammie began her career working for a NASA supplier, Rocketdyne, which built the engines for the space shuttles. She loved her job and never thought she would become a teacher. However, she began tutoring at a local

(Continued)

(Continued)

high school and the students hooked her. She went back to school to get a teaching degree and began teaching middle school science.

About ten years into her teaching career, she had a seventh-grade student who was bright, really into technology, but tough to engage in science. She describes how her teaching changed:

> One day I told the class, "Tonight you need to design a game to review cells." The next day the student handed me a thumb drive. He told me, "I hacked into Mario. All of the questions are on the coins. Kids jump up and get the coins. If they get the questions right, they get to keep them. If they get the questions wrong they fall into the pipes." All day long, kids I didn't even teach wanted to come in and play—before school, during lunch, and after school. I am not a gamer and I don't program, but I realized this is how my kids learn so this is how I need to teach.

Since then, Filament Games has enlisted her students' help in testing education games and her assistance as an expert consultant. She has started partnerships with multiple universities and code.org because her students wanted to start learning Python programming, and she knew she needed help. Her willingness to learn, take risks, and grow with her kids put her at the White House speaking at Game Jam about what her students were doing. She says, "I could not have connected these dots if I had planned it. I was just trying to serve kids." Last year, she became a Washington state regional science coordinator and says, "Now I get to serve students in fifty-nine districts." Tammie's novice mindset, coupled with her confidence and expertise, have taken her career in surprising directions, but her work is centered on making learning relevant for her kids. The only struggle she has is that her former students are writing so much code that they are overwhelming the school computer lab during lunch and after school hours—a great problem to have.

Give Students Choices

Students are no different than we are. A review of relevant studies shows that students value being treated with fairness, dignity, and individual respect (Hattie & Yates, 2014). We all want choices. With increasing knowledge and understanding, we all desire more autonomy (Deci & Flaste, 1995). Daniel Pink's book, *Drive* (2009), highlights our need to direct our own lives and create new things. If we can help tap into this internal drive and provide avenues for autonomy for our students, students can and will flourish.

Yes, most of us now teach to standards that are largely beyond our control, but there can still be latitude within those standards for our teaching and students' learning. For example, due to the accessibility of e-books, a proliferation of publishing options, and a global market, there are now more books available than at any point in the history of the world. Whether fiction or nonfiction, there are more options for students to read than I could have even imagined in the twentieth century when I started teaching.

In my experience, students, particularly in middle school through high school, need to feel like they are in control. Giving them options creates this perception—whether it is illusion or reality is irrelevant.

Give students options for the work they will do, books they will read, and essays they will write. Carol Ann Tomlinson (Tomlinson & Moon, 2013) has done a tremendous amount of work on different ways to differentiate through options for students such as RAFTs (Role, Audience, Format, Topic – See Box). Differentiating process, product, and content based on student interest and learning profile create space for individuals in a classroom.

Fearless Reflection

▶ RAFT

Role	Audience	Format	Topic
Booker T. Washington	U.S. House of Representatives	Five-minute speech	The education of youth
W.E.B. DuBois	Readers of the *New York Times*	Editorial	The education of youth

This is a simple RAFT but the beginning of numerous options for students. A student could mix and match these options to create an assignment of their choosing (e.g., W.E.B. DuBois could speak to the House or write an op-ed for the *Times* about the education of youth). This could be a speech given today, or one hundred years ago depending on the purpose of the assignment. Additional historical figures could be added on this same or related topic. Students have options that increase the likelihood of relevance that will improve the quality of their work and ultimately, their learning.

What is one assignment you could turn into a RAFT?

Doug Reeves (2011) suggests a menu approach to grading. At the beginning of a unit or semester, students are presented with a menu of assignments that have points attached to them. The menu includes the number of points needed to earn particular grades. Students determine which assignments they will complete to earn the number of points they desire. The teacher then scores the work and informs the student of the number of points earned. Students can do the work at school and at home. This could be more useful in particular subjects or grade levels, but it might be something to try in an upcoming unit. Like RAFTs, there is a significant amount of initial work for teachers to come up with the options, but once that work is done, then students are in control of their own work.

A Basic Example of a Menu Approach for an English Language Arts Unit on Humor

(Description, context, and rubrics would also be provided):

A = 90-100 points

B = 80-89 points

C = 70-79 points

Menu:

75 points: Essay comparing the techniques used by Shakespeare and Twain to communicate humor

50 points: Humorous five to seven minute presentation on the theory of humor in a selected text

50 points: A student-developed commercial for a book using a theory of humor in the commercial while highlighting the theory of humor in the book

25 points: Annotation of a student selected text identifying literary devices and imagery that communicate humor

20 points: Analysis with time stamps of devices used in a selected humorous YouTube speech

Establish and Uphold Consequences

Life is all about choices and consequences. I am a firm believer in consequences as opposed to punishments. "Punishment" connotes something that is being done to a student—something that is really out of the control of the one being punished. For some students, punishment separates the precipitating action from the punishment and is only negative. If however, we consider consequences, they can be positive or negative and flow naturally from choices. These consequences are extensions of the choices that students make. Our job as teachers then is to uphold the consequences that have been agreed upon by our classroom community.

We do not punish. We have all experienced teachers who punish the entire class for the behavior of the few with more menial work. Others will attempt to use grades punitively to dictate behavior. Both of these methods are problematic and decouple actions from consequences.

We uphold consequences. I use the term "uphold" here because I think it more accurately reflects what we do as compared to the typical term, "enforce," which sounds more punitive. In my experience, the most difficult part of upholding consequences is consistency. There are just some days when I am tired. I see a student doing poor work on a lab or lab report, and I just don't have the energy to try to refocus that student. However, I always regret this the next day when his work is even worse, or now his entire lab group is doing shoddy work.

Particularly for middle school and high school students, these consequences should be discussed and agreed upon at the beginning of the year. This is essential for them to have a sense of control. This is useful for younger students as well, but essential for students who are at higher levels of moral and cognitive development.

> Our job as teachers then is to uphold the consequences that have been agreed upon by our classroom community.

Punishment, humiliation, and sarcasm may elicit superficial compliance, but do not achieve real or lasting change. "In terms of managing your classroom, negative tactics are ultimately self-defeating. Compliance is not a strong educational goal, especially if achieved to the detriment of other more important educational goals" (Hattie & Yates, 2014, p. 18).

Negative consequences should be restorative in that the student should be earning a consequence that is just. For example, if a student disrupts class, instead of sending the student out into the hall which positively reinforces a negative behavior (student might not have wanted to be in class anyway), we need to find a way for the student to compensate for her disruption. In my science lab, I always kept a stack of dissection trays in the closet. These trays were not meticulously cleaned. When a student detracted from our class, she gave back to the class by spending some of her own time outside of class cleaning up dissection trays or anything that might have needed work for a proportionate amount of time. This was always discussed at the beginning of the year and fit my seventh graders' sense of justice.

Avoid Learned Helplessness

We want them to have a sense of self-efficacy, not learned helplessness. In the previous chapter, we established that learned helplessness is fostered when choices are decoupled from consequences in either a positive or negative way. If students recognize that they will be rewarded for bad choices (e.g., choice: students do not turn in homework, put forth effort, or demonstrate growth ➜ consequence: students receive As for substandard work),

Fearless Reflection

▶ Take a look at the table below. This is my interpretation of how consequences and punishments are different.

Consequences	Punishments
Natural	Artificial
Coupled with choices	Decoupled from choices
Student-driven	Teacher-driven
Restorative	Punitive
Positive and negative	Negative
Consistent	May seem random to students

Do you use consequences or punishment?

Is this just a semantic difference or do you see a substantive difference between them?

How effective and consistent are you with enforcing consequences?

then we have reinforced learned helplessness. Learned helplessness also develops from negative consequences for good choices (e.g., choice: working hard on a poster project at home without resources or parental help ➔ consequence: a low grade due to lack of effort because the project is not as "pretty" as other posters who had more parental support). Choices give students control over themselves and their work within reasonable parameters set by the teacher.

Learned helplessness is fostered when choices are decoupled from consequences in either a positive or negative way.

For example, we should not assign projects for work at home that are dependent on support and home resources. If the project is important for students to do, we should give them class time and adequate resources to do the work at school. Students' grades should not significantly improve because a parent could take them to a craft store. This type of a grade is not a reliable or valid measure of what students know. More importantly, the grade is unjust.

Upholding natural consequences is most beneficial. For example, if students fail to turn in work, then the work has to be done. At the discretion of the teacher, he may not give credit for this work, but the work must be completed. The work cannot be done during class time because every minute matters, so another time, before school, after school, or lunch will have to be used to complete the work. This is not punitive. The loss of time for the student to do something else is lost—a natural consequence of not completing work on time.

Of course consequences can be positive as well. Whenever possible, we should use more learning as the consequence for good choices. Providing students with homework passes and free time might motivate students to some extent but sends a problematic implicit message to students—if you do what you are supposed to do, you get to learn less.

I have used and observed several ways to make more learning the natural consequence of good work. In my seventh-grade science classroom, the last week of every quarter was devoted to extension labs that were not required by the curriculum. If

> Whenever possible, we should use more learning as the consequence for good choices.

you walked into our lab during those weeks, you would see students dissecting sheep hearts, making colloids, lowering the melting point of ice to create slushies, building cars powered by carbon dioxide cartridges, or anatomy/ physiology inquiry projects. Students were conducting tremendous scientific exploration.

In order to earn the opportunity to learn in this way, each team of students (four person teams all assigned a college team name and sitting under that pennant) had to earn one hundred points over the first eight weeks of the semester. Teams earned points for good lab work, teamwork, and through games. These points did not count toward grades. Points could also be lost for poor performance in those three areas. If teams did not earn their one hundred points, they spent the last week of the quarter in the library researching the concepts we were exploring in the lab. Each day, each student had to turn in a one to two page paper on the relevant concept.

How often did I have to enforce this negative consequence? Typically, one team would test my resolve on this during the first quarter. They would spend the week in the library dutifully writing about what other students were experiencing. I never had a group in the library after the first quarter. While the motivation I was providing was clearly extrinsic, by strategically using the subject itself, students were more likely to develop a level of appreciation for science that would lead to a more internalized desire for more learning.

I know of other teachers who did this far better. Hector Ibarra has a PhD in Science Education from the University of Iowa and has been on the Board of the National Assessment of Educational Progress. He is a brilliant scientist, and he uses that brilliance to hook his students on his subject. His students enter and win national science competitions from sponsors like eCybermission, Christopher Columbus Awards, Siemens, and Lexus. He spends many hours outside of class with his students exploring their ideas and inventions. His students love science and his inquiry-based approach. The consequence of their hard work has been over $700,000 in cash and savings bonds, and over $700,000 in program awards and travel expenses. This is over $1.4 million dollars for doing good science between 1993 and 2014. Hector is the epitome of an expert who continued to approach new ideas and concepts with a fresh perspective so that his students could do the same thing.

> This is over $1.4 million dollars for doing good science between 1993 and 2014.

Cultivating a Future-Orientation

Hector's students got a taste of what success derived from hard work looks and feels like. As teachers, this is one of the primary ways we can strategically motivate students by allowing them to see, taste, hear, and feel the payoff for hard work. Many "no excuses" charter schools use four-year colleges as the goal that will lead to a meaningful and satisfying career. Rooms and hallways are adorned with college pennants, college materials, and students are referred to as "scholars." College visits and bridge programs that create pre-K-20 partnerships and get students on college campuses can be beneficial for building a vision of the future.

Charter schools emphasize college, because graduating from college has an economic payoff. For adults ages 25-34 who work full time, those with a college degree earn $48,500 compared to those with only a high school degree who make $30,000 (U.S. Department of Education, National Center for Education Statistics, 2015 - see Figure 5.1). These data points could make for some interesting data analysis projects for our students.

> For adults ages 25-34 who work full time, those with a college degree earn $48,500 compared to those with only a high school degree who make $30,000.

Communicating the payoff of their hard work in our classes has to be about far more than economic benefit. Other than the delayed gratification, how much different is emphasizing how much money can be made than rewarding students with a Jolly Rancher for a correct answer? The payoff is really about how students will flourish if they work to their capacities. The key is to show students the possibilities that their untapped capacity can bring to fruition. Connecting them with professionals and more advanced students can allow students to catch a vision for what their lives could be

FIGURE 5.1 NCES's Report of Annual Earnings by Degree Attainment

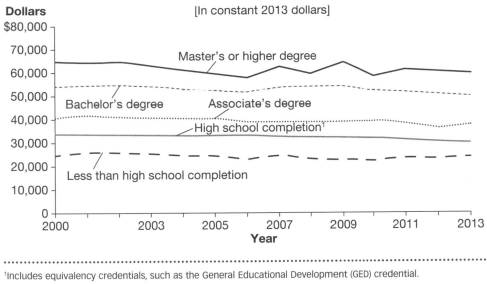

Median annual earnings of full-time year-round workers ages 25–34, by educational attainment: 2000–2013

¹Includes equivalency credentials, such as the General Educational Development (GED) credential.

SOURCE: U. S. Department of Education, National Center for Education Statistics (2015).

while bringing others alongside who can help them realize their best possible selves.

This is one particular area where career changers who have entered teaching through traditional or alternative routes can be tremendously beneficial. They have experienced other professions and can bring that expertise to older students. Career changers can also articulate why they have been drawn into teaching from other fields. If these teachers can help students connect the dots back to the work they are doing in school, this can become an ideal future-orientation as students move forward in their own self-discovery.

Tammie Schrader, the middle school science teacher profiled earlier, is a career changer whose previous experience impacts everything she does in the classroom. In her no-nonsense way, referring to her time building space shuttle engines, she says, "You want to talk some crazy crap? Try building a space shuttle. We were problem solving every day. So I have always taught open-ended and constructivist." She teaches her middle school students this way, and in so doing, she is teaching them the habits of mind that will make them successful problem solvers and critical thinkers in the future because her teaching is grounded in reality.

> If these teachers can help students connect the dots back to the work they are doing in school, this can become an ideal future-orientation as students move forward in their own self-discovery.

Fearless Reflection

▶ How would you rate your consistency in upholding consequences?

- 1 = "I can't be bothered with consequences."
- 10 = "I always uphold consequences."

1   2   3   4   5   6   7   8   9   10

What is challenging to you about upholding consequences?

What are some instances where you have had success in upholding consequences that have resulted in better student work and higher levels of student motivation?

How can you help your students see the long-term benefit of their hard work in your class?

What are some ways you can bring mentors and role models into your students' lives?

APPLY THE FOUR Rs TO MOTIVATION

As with everything in this book, apply the Four Rs to any new ideas for motivation. This is particularly important for motivation. Each student is unique. Each class has an ethos. Every teacher is an individual. Nothing will be motivational for everyone. I know high school teachers who use smencils (smelly pencils) and scratch-and-sniff stickers as rewards—whatever works. As teachers, we need to keep growing and recognize that this will be an annual if not hourly process of engaging and motivating students and ourselves.

So, now is your chance to keep your novice mindset and consider a couple of somewhat bizarre techniques I used

> Now is your chance to keep your novice mindset and consider a couple of somewhat bizarre techniques I used pragmatically to motivate both elementary and secondary students.

pragmatically to motivate both elementary and secondary students. Please read them critically, but keep your mind open as you may see opportunities to use something for your context. Some of my best ideas in the classroom started as seeds planted by a book, conversation, or professional development session. Those seeds grew into ideas that no one else would have recognized as having been derived from the original seed. Here are a few ideas that I hope will produce some seeds. These are examples of completely pragmatic approaches to strategic motivation—they are quirky extrinsic forms of motivation that worked for me.

Elvis as Master Motivator

In my fifth grade classroom, there was always a magnetic dress up Elvis on my front board. Although most of my students did not know who Elvis was, they certainly knew the magnetic dress up version on the board. That is because he held the fate of their Friday afternoon recess in his attire, or lack thereof. My students had a daily recess immediately after lunch, but Friday was an opportunity for a bonus recess just for our class. In our classroom, 5E, we would go out for the last fifteen minutes of the day as long as Elvis was still wearing all of his clothes including accessories like his lei and sunglasses.[1] If any of his clothes were missing, they lost minutes accordingly (e.g., lei missing = minus one minute, shoe missing = minus two minutes, shirt missing = minus three minutes, etc.).

I removed clothing throughout the week for poor transitions, indiscriminate noise, and off-task behavior of multiple groups of students. I wrote "forced" because I was merely upholding consequences. If the class was starting to get a bit out of hand, I took a couple of steps toward Elvis, and immediately urgent whispers of, "Mr. E.'s going for Elvis" could be heard across the room. Many times, those steps were all I needed. However, sometimes, I did have to remove an article of Elvis's clothes. Typically, this would bring back students' focus, and I did not have to say anything. If things were going well, the class could earn Elvis's clothes back for him.

This is really just a quirky version of a fairly common strategy. However, students knew how much I loved that recess time. This was our class time together to just have fun. We would all play a class game of kickball—everyone played. Typically we played boys vs. girls, and I always got to be on the girls' team. Not to brag, but we almost always won because we had some great girls, and I was an outstanding fifth grade kickball player at 6'4" tall and 220 pounds. This was class bonding time for us and was part of our identity. As a class, we were motivated to end our week enjoying being with each other.

Seating Charts, Bunsen Burners, and Burnt Marshmallows

In my science lab, I could not use kickball as an incentive. I also worried about what seventh graders would do with Elvis in a swimsuit on my board. Earlier

---

[1] To alleviate any potential alarm, Elvis was pictured in a swimsuit that could not be removed. I was not interested in dealing with sex education as a consequence of a motivational strategy.

in the chapter, I mentioned that I used points to determine if teams could participate in extension labs at the end of each quarter. However, I realized that if teams earned their one hundred points four weeks into the quarter, the points had no power to motivate students to perform well. Therefore, I linked their points to two incentives. The first was that the teams got to select their seat for the next quarter based on the number of points they earned. For many middle and high school students, who is on their team or is their lab partner could be the most important part of science to them. Instead of spending hours trying to come up with combinations that could work that invariably failed to meet my needs or their desires, this method allowed them to choose. There were two rules and one guiding principle that governed their choices:

1. You cannot sit with anyone that is currently on your team.

2. The teacher always has veto power.

Governing principle: Choose wisely. Who will you work well with? Your team's success is dependent on how well you work together, not who your friend is—a friend who might end up being a distraction.

This method of seating worked effectively as an incentive and as a management device. Because they wanted to sit where they had chosen, they had an incentive to work well together.

The second incentive for moving beyond one hundred points as a team was a cheap, quirky reward. Many science teachers would never do this because science labs are for careful observation, experimentation bounded by safety precautions, and serious work. This was our only exception to those norms and the only time food was allowed in the lab, and we still maintained a safe environment. The team in each class that earned the most points in a quarter got to come to the lab during lunch and make s'mores. We roasted/torched marshmallows over the Bunsen burners and then placed them on the obligatory graham crackers and chocolate. Bunsen burners are terrible for roasting marshmallows because they burn too hot, but students enjoyed them that much more.

> Whatever it takes to give students "autonomy, complexity, and a connection between effort and reward" we need to do in order to help the work of school become satisfying.

Whatever it takes to give students "autonomy, complexity, and a connection between effort and reward" we need to do in order to help the work of school become satisfying. Teachers at all levels must determine what is motivating in their classroom cultures—quirky can always work if the teacher creates the right culture. This requires creativity, innovation, and a willingness to learn alongside our students. In the end, we want to demand a great deal from ourselves and our students, so that they will demand the same from themselves. That is the practice we will examine in the next chapter with our novice mindset.

Key Takeaways and Fearless Practices

- Your students are motivated by autonomy, complexity, and the connection between effort and reward.

- You cannot intrinsically motivate your students.

- Avoid short-sighted extrinsic motivation.

- You can help students tap into motivation that could be intrinsic or at least, delayed extrinsic motivation.

- Making learning relevant—your decisions are always based on your students' needs.

- We all want choices—give them to students whenever possible.

- Choices for assessment can become effective differentiation (e.g., RAFTs and menus).

- Do not punish. Establish consequences with your students to maintain and restore a culture of learning.

- Have the perseverance to consistently uphold consequences.

- Foster equity in your classroom by ensuring that all students have the opportunity to succeed and never grade work done by parents.

- The best reward for good choices should be more learning.

- Cultivate a future-orientation by showing students how their hard work can pay off for them.

- Use whatever works for you to motivate students (e.g., Elvis, s'mores, and seating charts).

Open-Ended Case Studies

Select one of the teacher case studies below and answer the associated questions.

- Think back to Graham in the first chapter. As a first-year teacher, he used class money, "skrilla," that would be used in a Friday auction to see who would be that week's "skrillionaire." Students earned "skrilla" by demonstrating the character traits that they emphasized as a class each week. That resulted in students having their pictures taken with his alter ego, and the honor of keeping a Captain America statue on their desk the following week. What type of motivation is this? What does this cost Graham? What kind of application could this have in your class?

- You are a high school math teacher and you primarily teach seniors. You see 160 students per day. You teach one AP class, but the majority of your students want to be done with high school—especially math. For about 75 percent of your students, grades and homework are not motivating. Is there a use for "skrilla," magnetic Elvises, point systems, or burnt marshmallows as motivational gimmicks? What can you do that might strategically motivate students? Hint—there is a chapter coming on building strategic relationships. Beyond building relationships, how could you make your class relevant or provide your students with a meaningful future-orientation?

Reflect

- As a student, in which classes were you most motivated to learn? What did these classes have in common?

- Knowing that we are all egocentric, how will you move beyond your own personal preferences to motivate your students?

- How have you handled choices and consequences in your classroom? What has worked? Why?

- What is the most successful thing you have done to help students develop a future-orientation? Why was it successful?

Risk: 3-2-1 Action Steps

3:   Identify three things you could adapt that would make your class more relevant for your students.

Possible steps:

- Examine the process by which students acquire skills and knowledge in your class. Identify ways to allow for more collaboration and autonomy.

- Take one assignment and contextualize it in three different ways. Give students a choice of which assignment they will complete.

- Survey students about which assignments they find to be most relevant. Determine if there are ways to increase these types of assignments.

2:   Find two ways to help your students develop a future-orientation.

Possible steps:

- Invite a former student to come back and talk to your class about the benefits of working hard and growing in this classroom.

- Discuss delayed gratification with your students. Help them identify why it is so challenging, and then help them see why it is so rewarding.

1: Implement one pragmatic idea that will increase motivation

Possible steps

- Identify one of your quirkiest interests or a quirky interest of your students. Determine a way to use that as a reward for hard work.

- Determine the most engaging activity in your classroom. Figure out how students could get more time doing this as a reward for quality work.

Revise or Reject

After taking a risk, determine what to do next. Was it worthy of revision or rejection?

☐ Reject   ☐ Revise

Write down a few notes about what worked, what did not, and what you might change.

CHAPTER 6

Expect More

"She was mean out of the kindness of her heart."

Philadelphia student referring to a "good teacher"
(Wilson & Corbett, 2001, p. 91)

Most teachers do not want to be "mean." This is especially true for new teachers who are more likely to fall into the trap of trying to be students' friends. I ask my preservice teachers, "How many of you would like for a student to say you were 'mean out of the kindness of [your] heart'?" The majority of them look at me like I am crazy. However, there are always a few who understand what this student means and say that they would take this as a compliment. My confidence in those students as future teachers increases significantly. They recognize what Wilson and Corbett (2001) report hearing from interviews with urban students: teachers who are demanding communicate love and respect. Those who are not demanding communicate lack of care and disrespect. In this case, "mean" is synonymous with strict and demanding.

> Teachers who are demanding communicate love and respect.

These are some ideas that the novice teachers with whom I work need to own:

- Students do not need us to be their friends. They need us to be their teachers.

- Students do not need to be entertained. They need to be engaged in meaningful work.

- Students do not need to like us. They need to respect us.

- Teachers do not always have to like their students (it certainly helps), but teachers have to love them.

Most of my preservice teachers will assent to all of these statements with their heads, but in their hearts they believe they can be demanding, *and* be friends, entertaining, like and be liked at the same time. Sometimes this is true; however, there are times when it is not and at those times, we have to choose the tougher road.

We have empirical evidence that the tougher road is the right one. The Bill & Melinda Gates Foundation invested more than $45 million in the Measures of Effective Teaching (MET) Project (Kane, Kerr, & Pianta, 2014). As part of that project, they used the Tripod Survey designed by Harvard researcher Ron Ferguson. Tripod is a student survey that measures different practices of effective teaching. Simply put, Tripod examines the "7 Cs:" caring, controlling, clarifying, challenging, captivating, conferring, and consolidating.

Fearless Reflection

▶ Ron Ferguson's Tripod Survey identifies seven teaching practices of effective teaching:

Caring about students (nurturing productive relationships)

Controlling behavior (promoting cooperation and peer support)

Clarifying ideas and lessons (making success seem feasible)

Challenging students to work hard and think hard (pressing for effort and rigor)

Captivating students (making learning interesting and relevant)

Conferring (eliciting students' feedback and respecting their ideas)

Consolidating (connecting and integrating ideas to support learning)

- Of these seven Cs, which do you think is the most important for effective teaching?

If you were like most teachers with whom I share these seven practices, you would probably say caring. However, if you recognize the chapter you are currently reading you might be more likely to say something else.

The MET Project used the Tripod Survey, five different teaching observation tools including the ubiquitous Danielson Framework, and value-added measures of student achievement. Value-added measures are used when a student's growth is calculated based on test performance over time (e.g., comparing student growth on a sixth-grade standardized achievement test to a seventh-grade test while taking into account the progress other similar students have made). Using the Tripod survey and Danielson Framework results, the researchers found that "challenge" or "press," not "care," most strongly predicted value-added growth for students (Ferguson & Danielson, 2014). In the next chapter, we will further unpack these findings and see that more is needed than just "press," but for now, we will explore ways

> The researchers found that "challenge" or "press," not "care," most strongly predicted value-added growth for students.

to effectively demand as much as possible from our students.

Effective teachers must be demanding of both their students and themselves while still communicating care and compassion. This is more important than ever, as positional authority and respect are no longer automatically granted to teachers. Novices work very hard in their first few years of teaching but sometimes lose sight of the need to be demanding out of a desire to be liked. Maybe you are a new teacher anticipating entering this stage, or a more experienced teacher who can remember back to this stage. If a desire to be liked by students supplants a desire to be respected, then we become less demanding and can inadvertently end up enabling students. This creates that same sense of learned helplessness we discussed in the previous chapter. Conversely, by modeling a strong work ethic and demanding a similar work ethic from our students, teachers gain credibility and student outcomes improve (Ferguson & Danielson, 2014; Kane et al., 2014). In order to be lovingly demanding to maximize growth, teachers and students must be honest and transparent.

HONESTY AND TRANSPARENCY: THE MARKERS OF EFFECTIVE ASSESSMENT

Being demanding is largely about being honest with our students. To do that, we must start by being honest with ourselves. Madeline Hunter, an influential twentieth century educator, said, "To say you have taught when no one has learned is to say you sold when no one bought." For most of us, this is an extremely obvious statement, but without student assessment, we operate as if learning is decoupled from teaching.

> Without student assessment, we operate as if learning is decoupled from teaching.

To be completely transparent is vulnerable. For example, what is the best indicator of my ability to teach preservice teachers? Their ability to teach students, right? I am encouraged when I see my students become teachers who do amazing things with their students. I am discouraged and question my efficacy when that does not occur. Teaching is a complex task, and I certainly cannot take credit for the effective teachers who have gone through our program, but I do need to assess their progress toward effective teaching from where they begin in my classes to their work with their own students. We post as much data as we can on www.wheteach.org that reports where our graduates are working, how they rate their preparation, and how they rate their effectiveness.

▶ How tightly coupled is *your* (*italicized* so we don't get hung up on standardized assessment) assessment of student learning to your teaching?

- 1 = "My assessments of student learning is completely unrelated to my teaching."
- 10 = "My assessments of student learning encompasses my effectiveness as a teacher."

1	2	3	4	5	6	7	8	9	10

What makes you uncomfortable about coupling assessment of student learning to your teaching?

Who is someone that you trust to give you honest feedback about your teaching?

- Can you be honest with him or her with your assessment of student learning?

- Is the relationship based on reciprocal trust?

Avoid "Fake Teaching"

When I first started teaching, I did a lot of what I call, "fake teaching." Fake teaching is the opposite of visible learning (Hattie, 2012). Hopefully you have not experienced fake teaching, but if you have, you know it.

In my first few years in the classroom, I was excited about everything. I spent hours planning activities, games, simulations, learning experiences, and presentations. We studied Mesopotamia, force and motion, novels, and fractions with passion. We even had something called Prairie Day (not my idea, but yes, in Illinois we celebrate large flat areas of unmowed grass) where students came dressed as "prairie people," and we worked with another teacher's antique tools and school supplies. I taught a lot of stuff. We did a lot of stuff. Students were happy. Parents were happy. My principal was happy.

However, I began to have uneasy feelings about my teaching. I would get to the ends of units and wonder what I should test students over so I could give them a grade. I would then create a test, unit project, or paper that would address many of the themes we had addressed through the unit. Most students "earned" A's or B's on the assessments. Students were happy. Parents were happy. My principal was happy. I was on to the next round of activity planning with plenty of vigor, but with little understanding of actual student learning.

Fake Teaching vs. Hattie's Visible Learning Mind Frames for Teachers

Fake Teaching: "I don't want to know my impact, because I might not like what I find"	Visible Learning: "Know thy impact"
1. My fundamental task is to maintain the appearance of control and good teaching.	1. My fundamental task is to evaluate the effect of my teaching on students' learning and achievement.
2. The success of my students is dependent on how interested they are in what I am doing and the grades my assessments produce.	2. The success and failure of my students' learning is about what I do or don't do. I am a change agent.
3. I talk more about teaching than learning.	3. I want to talk more about learning than teaching.
4. Assessment is about a grade to report to parents and students.	4. Assessment is about my impact.
5. I teach through dialogue or monologue—whatever is easiest to control.	5. I teach through dialogue not monologue.
6. I always "do my best."	6. I enjoy the challenge and never retreat to "doing my best."
7. It's my role to develop positive relationships with students, colleagues, and parents—by making sure everyone likes me.	7. It's my role to develop positive relationships in class and staffrooms.
8. I ensure everyone knows that my students are happy and I am competent.	8. I ensure everyone knows the language of learning.

In my fourth year, I read the first edition of *Understanding by Design* (Wiggins & McTighe, 1998). Although widely used today, the basic premise of the book was an epiphany for me. Teachers should teach essential understandings through essential questions—a completely new way of thinking for me. What really blew my mind was that assessments—diagnostic, formative, self, and summative assessments—should be designed before any lessons. Wiggins and McTighe describe this as backward design. This transformed my teaching because I was reoriented to be more focused on learning.

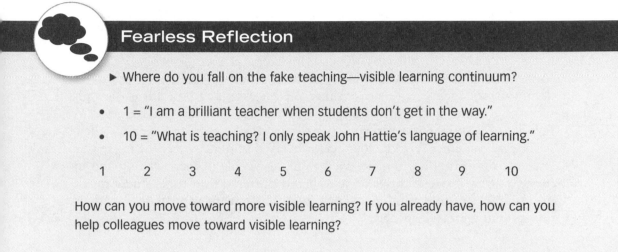

Fearless Reflection

▶ Where do you fall on the fake teaching—visible learning continuum?

- 1 = "I am a brilliant teacher when students don't get in the way."

- 10 = "What is teaching? I only speak John Hattie's language of learning."

1   2   3   4   5   6   7   8   9   10

How can you move toward more visible learning? If you already have, how can you help colleagues move toward visible learning?

Self-Assessment

If you have lost your novice mindset, self-assessment is the quickest way to get it back. Start owning where your students are growing and not growing. Take this one step further and help your students own their learning through self-assessment. Quality self-assessment means moving beyond students apathetically completing a rubric that they do not understand. We can do better than having students complete an exit slip with a question they still have, but do not really care about, when we know those questions will not be answered. I am embarrassed to admit that I was one of those teachers that sometimes used rubrics and exit slips in this way to be able to say that students had assessed themselves. Frequently, these kinds of self-assessment practices are mindless compliance exercise. Meaningful self-assessment requires students to honestly reflect on their own learning and progress. When they have done this, we can help them become more demanding of themselves. The question is, how do we make self-assessment thoughtful and more than a compliance exercise?

Learning targets are one way to get students into meaningful self-assessment. If our goal, teachers and students, is to learn a lesson-sized concept or lesson-sized skill, then at the end of that lesson students should be able to assess their progress toward that outcome. If this becomes a daily routine, this process becomes natural and is not just another activity to check off of a list of good teaching practices. Performing arts teachers and their students provide outstanding examples of meaningful self-assessment. Each fall semester, I get the opportunity to work with orchestra, band, and choral music student teachers. When we start to discuss assessment, they look at me kind of funny. It is a quizzical look that seems to say, "Well how else would I know if they were getting better if I did not listen and did not ask them to listen to themselves?" For them, teaching is entirely about what their students perform and how they improve. Their goal is to get musicians hearing and correcting mistakes without having to be redirected. Needless to say, this is not how all teachers view their own teaching.

Another way to engage students in meaningful self-assessment is to require them to track their progress over time. The easiest way to do this is through writing. Requiring multiple drafts of work where students are required to revise and capture those revisions is a useful way for them to see how their work evolves. Since writing goes across every discipline, we can all give our students opportunities to make their thinking visible in their writing and in the ways they revise. If this is done well and captured over time, students can see the tracks of their thinking, which should help them appreciate how their understanding has deepened.

Diagnostic, Formative, and Summative Assessment

We have not fully tapped the potential of diagnostic, formative, and summative assessment as a profession. There are well-researched and extensive treatments of these forms of assessments (e.g., Black, Harrison, Marshall, & William, 2004; Popham, 2008; Reeves, 2011; Wiggins & McTighe, 2005), but I will briefly address how we can more effectively use assessment to be more demanding.

Diagnostic, or preassessment, happens before a unit is taught. In fact, diagnostic assessment should happen weeks before a unit is taught. Some teachers realize that diagnostic assessment is something they should do or are required to do by administration, so they comply by conducting some kind of pretest on the first day of the unit. Generally speaking, this dooms the diagnostic assessment to be a complete waste of time that will only breed cynicism of students over time. As students, we all experienced pretests that had absolutely no bearing on what we were taught (e.g., the student who gets 95 percent of the answers right on the pretest and proceeds through the unit in exactly the same manner as the student who gets 12 percent of the answers right.). Giving the preassessment well before the unit is taught, gives us some time to adjust instruction for individual needs. Without the additional time, we set ourselves up for failure and decrease the likelihood that we will actually be demanding.

Formative assessment is feedback—an essential element of deliberate practice. How do we know students are learning while we are teaching? Feedback can be what we get from students—answers to questions, drowsiness, lack of engagement, formal, or informal. Feedback is different than advice and evaluation (Wiggins, 2012). Most of what we provide as demanding teachers is formative feedback. This can be immediate (e.g., "You need to project your voice" or "Can you explain a bit more about that?") or it can be delayed (e.g., written feedback on a paper or project that will be resubmitted).

Teachers and students do not want advice on what they have done wrong. Instead, they want feedback on how they can improve (Hattie & Yates, 2014). When this becomes the purpose of assessment, everything changes.

Fearless Reflection

▶ I fear that most of my feedback to my preservice teachers leans toward advice—"This could be more clear. This learning target is not observable. This explanation of the science concept is unclear." All of it may be true, but it does not rise to what Grant Wiggins describes as feedback. Feedback should have the following seven elements (Wiggins, 2012):

Goal-Referenced: Remind students of the goal of the work and then ask questions or give feedback that reorients them. Example: The goal of this writing assignment is to persuade your reader. When you revise this piece, ask yourself: Is this persuasive? Is my thesis clear? Do I have enough supporting evidence?

Tangible and Transparent: Goal-oriented feedback needs to be clear to students. Wiggins recounts a classic example of feedback that is opaque. A student approaches his teacher at the end of the year and says, "You kept writing this same word on my English papers all year, and I still don't know what it means." The teacher asked what the word was. "Vag-oo," he said. The word was "vague."

Actionable: A letter grade and a "well done" are not actionable feedback. Students need to know what they can do to improve.

User-Friendly: Effective feedback is specific, concrete, and understandable. For instance, I am a terrible golfer. Recently a golf pro took on the unenviable task of helping my golf swing. He gave me one simple piece of feedback to work on for forty-five minutes. Now I am a slightly less terrible golfer.

Timely: There is always a tension between detail and specificity and time. We all know that there are diminishing returns on feedback as time passes. We need to set up opportunities to train students to give one another feedback or determine ways to expedite our feedback process to ensure that it is timely.

Ongoing: Give students timely feedback that allows them to adjust their performance and try again. Think Angry Birds for the classroom—almost immediate feedback with opportunities for revision.

(Continued)

(Continued)

Consistent: Feedback must be stable and accurate. Training students to give each other feedback and highly descriptive rubrics can be helpful to this end.

Progress Toward a Goal: Orienting feedback toward long-term goals can be helpful here. Formative feedback should help students see how they are progressing toward those goals.

How good are you at giving feedback as opposed to advice or evaluation?

- 1 = "I write 'Good Job' on every paper."
- 10 = "I am Grant Wiggins, feedback guru."

| 1 | 2 | 3 | 4 | 5 | 6 | 7 | 8 | 9 | 10 |

Feedback, like differentiation, is a concept that can overwhelm teachers. How can you give better feedback without taking additional time?

True summative assessment is rare in demanding teachers' classrooms. Summative assessment indicates finality—a summation of learning. Most of our assessments will build on one another and are therefore, formative. In my science classes, students were never done with my end-of-unit "summative" assessments until they had earned an 80 percent. The class would move on to new concepts, but over their lunches students would return to my lab to attack the previous unit in new ways. Some students would spend three weeks of lunches in my labs mastering the previous knowledge and skills. They would go through as many as seven to eight versions of the test until they got to an 80 percent. I did average all of the scores for their final grade because I wanted students to do well the first time if possible. Were these truly "summative" assessments? In my class, we were always building on prior units, so I don't really think so. There were two assessments that were summative for my science students: a final exam I gave in mid-February after we had completed all of the standards for seventh grade[1] and the state assessment that came every April.[2]

---

[1] We spent the rest of the year exploring science concepts that went beyond the state requirements—we actually did some great science beyond creating flammable lava lamps. At the time the state standards were not particularly rigorous.

[2] Standardized assessments do not come close to fully measuring the impact of a teacher even with value-added calculations. That said, my students' value-added scores allowed me wide latitude in my classroom (Eckert, 2016; Eckert & Dabrowski, 2010)

Good assessment is the mark and method of the demanding teacher. However, we are not always quick to value assessment in this way due to our skepticism about the accountability culture in which we reside.

Good assessment is the mark and method of the demanding teacher.

This became clear to me in a conversation I had with a student teacher in a high school science placement. For twelve weeks he cotaught an honors physics class and a lower level physical science class. The district administered a local assessment at the beginning of the year and at the end of the first semester for both classes. The students in the honors physics course doubled their scores on the semester exam when compared to the preassessment. The students in the lower level physical science course scored lower on their semester exam than they did on the preassessment.

Red flags, sirens, buzzers, anything to indicate a problem should be erupting in our minds. However, they weren't for this student teacher. When I asked the student teacher to explain, he told me that he had only taught the physical science class full time for four weeks. When I asked him to explain how students took the exact same test after a full semester of instruction and knew less at the end of the semester, he offered three explanations:

"The test is really old."

"The test isn't very good."

"The students are not very motivated."

All three explanations could be true, but none of them explained how they would have done worse on a second administration after a semester of alleged learning. I asked him how they had done on unit exams and in labs. He explained, "The students like the teacher because he understands that they don't love physical science. They don't do a lot of labs and they always do okay on the tests because he curves the scores. He has to because the average score is usually about 30 percent."

So much is wrapped up in that explanation, but the key is the assessment issue. This cooperating teacher knew students were not learning and had developed a system to produce grades that ranked how little students knew in comparison to one another. This is not demanding, transparent, honest, or useful. This is the type of context where students could spend months in a class and know less at the end of that semester than they did at the beginning.

GIVE STUDENTS A CHANCE TO GROW

Growth might have been possible in that physical science classroom for some students, but this certainly was not the expectation. Students tend to grow where growth is the expectation. We have known this since the often-cited "Pygmalion in the Classroom" study. In this study, at the beginning of the school year teachers were told that 20 percent of their students had done extremely well on an aptitude test. At the end of the year, those students demonstrated greater gains on IQ and achievement tests than the other students in the same classrooms. We might expect this of the high achieving 20 percent, right? However, the original aptitude test was fictitious and in fact, the students comprising the "high expectations" group were a randomly selected group of students of varying IQ scores.

The problem is that almost all teachers believe they hold high expectations for their students. Sometimes those high expectations are conditioned by phrases such as, "I have high expectations for *these* students," or, "This is the most you can expect from *this* group." In these statements, we see a tacit lowering of expectations. However, there are some teachers that hold expectations for students that seem so high they seem outlandish. Famous teaching examples include Jaime Escalante and Rafe Esquith, but there are many more not-so-famous examples like Hector Ibarra, Laura Fittz, and Ben Jimenez.

Jaime Escalante was made famous in the movie *Stand and Deliver* for believing that under-served English learners could do well in AP calculus. Most people did not believe this was possible. But he did and demanded more from students than they believed they had. In 1982, his 18 students did so well on the AP Calculus exam that 14 of the students were accused of cheating by the Educational Testing Service and 12 retook the exam. All of them passed. By 1987, only four schools in the country had more students taking and passing the AP Calculus exam than Garfield High (Woo, 2010). Escalante did not do this alone. Ben Jimenez is an award winning calculus teacher. Never heard of him, right? He just happened to teach at Garfield High along with Jaime Escalante. Like many stories of superhero teachers, it seems that these amazing, charismatic teachers work alone. Escalante might have been *The Best Teacher in America* (Matthews, 1988), but he had a remarkably supportive principal and taught with Jimenez (Woo, 2010).

Rafe Esquith (2003, 2007) holds similarly high expectations for his students. Like Escalante, he teaches under-served English learners in Los Angeles, but his students are fifth graders. Each year, his students travel the country performing full Shakespearean plays that they have memorized and fully understand. I taught fifth-grade students for seven years, and did not even imagine that most of my students could even read Shakespeare, let alone memorize, perform, and understand his works. This challenges many of my assumptions about fifth graders. Did I really expect as much as I could have from my fifth graders?

Hector Ibarra is the science teacher who was mentioned in the last chapter. His expectations and his middle school students' hard work resulted in over $1.4 million for his students through science competitions and scholarship programs. Much of this occurred in his classroom, but he also spent considerable time outside of his classroom with his students. Most of us have never even heard of their amazing work or tried to replicate it with our students.

Even more quietly, there are teachers working in our schools who are demanding a great deal from their students. Laura Fittz is a third-year teacher at Glencliff High School in Nashville. Although she will be the first to acknowledge the challenges that come with being a novice teacher in an under-served urban high school, she effervesces when she talks about what her students are doing. She teaches high school boys who are excited about English. She says, "I am so proud of them [her students]. They are working so hard for me. My boys got really engaged in a spoken word poem assignment, and I learned so much about them. Now they are really writing." She can hardly contain her pride in their work, as she shows the online video of student performances to anyone willing to watch.

These examples are encouraging. Some of them are higher profile than others, but I am more encouraged by the examples about which we have not heard. This gives me hope that more teachers are giving their students a chance to grow.

Fearless Reflection

▶ How high are your expectations? Be honest!

- 1 = "My students don't care. Why should I?"
- 10 = "Esquith and Escalante treat their students like toddlers compared to me."

1	2	3	4	5	6	7	8	9	10

Who do you know who has high expectations for students? How do they communicate this?

Having truly high expectations for students is challenging. How have you met that challenge?

- How do you give your students a chance to grow?

- What constrains your students' growth?

- What constrains your willingness to give students a chance to grow?

TECHNIQUES THAT PROMOTE STUDENT GROWTH

Only accept students' best work: This is a tough one to get started, but when we do, life is so much better. For papers, projects, or major assignments, we cannot accept the work if we know the student can do better. We return the work and communicate the belief that the student is capable of more. If the student is not certain how to improve, we provide constructive feedback. For most students, work quality will dramatically improve on subsequent assignments if they know they cannot slide by. I have experienced the consequences of this kind of improved quality and also what happens when I have accepted lower quality work. Students do not want a critical breakdown of what they did wrong. They want feedback on how they can improve (Hattie & Yates, 2014). This takes time on the part of the teacher but will pay dividends in improved student work.

No zeros: This is a recommendation from Doug Reeves (2011). By the time many students reach middle school and high school, zeros for work that is not submitted mean very little. If students have learned over the course of years that they will receive zeros for not turning in work and then continue to progress through the system even with failing grades, they have internalized learned helplessness—their actions are not affecting consequences. Zeros also have a disproportionate effect in grading scales that consider anything from 0–60 percent to be failing. The consequence for not completing work should be completing the work. Giving a zero gives tacit approval to not learning if the student is not motivated by grades.

Everyone answers: Doug Lemov (2010, 2015) refers to this as the "no opt out" technique. If we truly believe that everyone can learn, then everyone must be given an opportunity to answer questions and participate. In Chapter 4, we explored wait time one (three seconds after asking a question) and wait time two (three seconds after a student answers), as well as ways to engage the entire classroom. For this to work for all students, all students need to have an opportunity to answer. If the student does not know the answer, then we move to another student who does. We then return to the first student, and she gives us the answer that she just heard or builds upon it. It is fine if a student does not know an answer initially. By returning to that student, we communicate that she is capable of knowing the answer and cannot mentally check out of class.

These are just techniques. Whether or not they will work for us depends on how we communicate expectations and provide support for our students. In other words, how can we be "warm demanders?"

BE A WARM DEMANDER

When students know we are demanding because we care about them, they will respond. Researchers refer to these kinds of teachers as "warm demanders" (Bondy & Ross, 2008; Bondy, Ross, Hambacher, & Acosta, 2012). These teachers, typically in urban environments, embrace being "strict," "tough," and "mean" because they believe that this is synonymous with being demanding. Researchers have shown that coupling academic press (demanding) with support (warmth) is the best way to improve student learning and long-term outcomes.

> Researchers have shown that coupling academic press (demanding) with support (warmth) is the best way to improve student learning and long-term outcomes.

Teachers communicate support through caring relationships, engaging and respectful lessons, listening, and availability (Ferguson & Danielson, 2014).

The way we communicate demand and support is dependent upon our contexts and teaching personas. The way we communicate high expectations and support will vary within schools and certainly between school populations. Included in our consideration are gender, race, and background of the teacher and students. Moreover, the way an introvert and an extrovert communicate love for students and demand their best work will vary. Because of this, I can offer only a few pragmatic suggestions without knowing you or your context. I encourage you to explore further what being a warm demander might look like for you in your context.

Figure 6.1 is a 2x2 designed to help us think about ourselves related to Ferguson and Danielson's findings on press and support. The upper right quadrant is where we want to be—providing support and press. Some of us might provide support but are not providing academic press, while others might be demanding without support. If we do not provide support and are not demanding, then we fall in the bottom left quadrant, which is the most problematic. Consider this 2x2 within your specific context. Where do you fall? Where might you need to grow?

What follows are two ways to be lovingly demanding with regard to two of the most challenging aspects of teaching for novices and veterans alike: student discipline and standardized tests.

Deal With Issues in Your Classroom

Particularly for novice teachers, student behavior can challenge their self-efficacy. Students can

FIGURE 6.1 Support and Academic Press 2×2

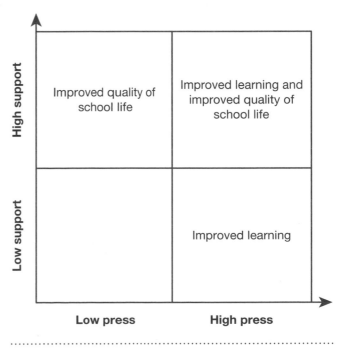

be insubordinate, belligerent, defiant, apathetic, or withdrawn. Sometimes students communicate disrespect toward teachers or each another. Our response is typically dependent on the degree of the disrespect and conspicuousness of the action. In a classroom predicated on choices and consequences, there should be clear guidelines for responses that will mitigate the disrespect. Sometimes those consequences include sending students to a dean or the principal. Most of the time, that is a mistake. I make this claim with the caveat that in instances of physical violence, sexual harassment, or other extreme situations, sending students to deans or principals will be the best course of action.

However, when we send students out of the classroom to be dealt with by someone else, we tacitly communicate that we cannot handle the situation. This erodes student respect for us, and it erodes the classroom community. The opportunity for the consequence to be a learning experience for the student and the class might be lost.

> When we send students out of the classroom to be dealt with by someone else, we tacitly communicate that we cannot handle the situation.

Additionally, learning stops for the student if he is in the hall or in the principal's office. Exclusion from learning is a problematic consequence, even if it is unintended. If we are demanding and treat every minute of class time as valuable, then we should be very reticent to cause students to miss any time. If we exclude the student and he wants to miss class time then we have positively reinforced a negative behavior. Part of being demanding is demonstrating that class time is precious and anything that arises in class that causes students to not work to their potential will be dealt with in class. This might mean that an issue will be dealt with after class, but as much as possible, we should handle this ourselves and not outsource it.

I would extend this principle further and apply it to contacting home as a consequence for bad choices. In many elementary school classrooms, this is the most severe consequence possible for students. Engaging with parents is extremely valuable for teachers and students. Once we know our parents, communicating challenges their children present and face can be tremendously valuable as a means of finding solutions. However, having students "call home" as the ultimate consequence for poor choices sends a similar message as sending a student to the office. We are outsourcing the consequence. Not only does this imply that we cannot handle issues that arise in the classroom, contacting home with the hope that consequences will be enforced at home can result in unintended consequences.

In my second year of parent-teacher conferences, I mentioned a minor incident that had happened earlier that week to the parent of one of my students. The father responded rather ominously, "We will deal with that as soon as we get home." A bit concerned, I assured him that the student had already earned a consequence and that we had not had any more issues. He assured me, "I know how to handle my son."

The next day, the student would not make eye contact with me when he gave me a handshake at the door to the classroom. He was withdrawn in the morning, and I had a distinct sense that things had gone badly the night before. At lunch I pulled the student aside and asked what was wrong. He never told me about the previous night, but with tears brimming in his eyes, he asked, "Why did you tell my dad what happened? I had already gotten a consequence here."

Communication with parents is vital, but when incidents arise in the classroom we should attempt to uphold natural consequences whenever possible. If we are going to be warm demanders then we must be the ones to do the demanding and provide the supports even when it means upholding consequences. Depending on the grade level and incident, parents should be informed of choices and consequences, but we should not expect the parents to be responsible for upholding consequences for choices made in our classrooms.

Fearless Reflection

▶ If you have not already, plot where you fall on the 2x2 in Figure 6.1.

- Do you need to increase support, press, or both?

- What are some issues that might arise that must go to a dean or a principal?

- What are some issues that will require parental engagement?

- What are some areas where teachers turn to administrators or parents to solve classroom issues that could be addressed in the classroom?

Use Standardized Tests to Your Advantage

Very few teachers I know think of standardized testing as being advantageous. For the first eight years of my teaching career, I saw them as a necessary annoyance. I would give the tests each spring and look at the results each fall. Each year, the story was basically the same: I had pretty good kids who did pretty well. Students were "proficient" or "advanced" and parents and administrators were happy.

Then I moved to Tennessee to teach science to middle school students, coach girls' and boys' basketball, girls' and boys' tennis, and start a doctorate at Vanderbilt University. Standardized tests became a tremendous professional asset for me.

Tennessee has had the longest running value-added assessment system of any state in the country (TVAAS). The idea is

> Standardized tests became a tremendous professional asset for me.

simple (Sanders & Horn, 1994), yet controversial (American Statistical Association, 2014): based on students' previous performance on standardized tests, how would we predict that they would perform? Once this has been determined by TVAAS, students' actual performance is compared to the predicted trajectory (Sanders & Horn, 1994).

Simply put, my tests and labs were significantly more difficult than the state assessment upon which my value-added scores were based. Remember, all of my students had to earn an 80 percent on each unit exam before moving ahead. I could be extremely demanding because I had very capable students. At the time, neither the Tennessee science standards nor assessment were particularly rigorous. Because my students consistently mastered the requisite seventh-grade skills and knowledge by the middle of February, we had the rest of the year to explore other areas of science together. We continued to work hard, but they took over much of the learning. I had teams of students who served as lab assistants for each class. They set up labs, cleaned up labs, and even created lab safety videos for us. We conducted student-driven inquiry projects and extension labs. My time teaching students was my refuge from all of the other work that I faced outside the classroom. That space was created by my students' value-added scores as they were showing gains that exceeded the scores required to earn a value-added "A" from the state by magnitudes of fifteen to twenty times (Eckert, 2016; Eckert & Dabrowski, 2010).

We know that standardized test scores cannot encompass all that occurs in a classroom. We cannot allow them to constrain what our students do. Instead, we should push our students to move beyond these requirements and whenever possible, use those scores to create space in our rooms for creativity and exploration. As we do this, we can work to build the important relationships that will move beyond higher test scores to greater learning and inspiration.

Key Takeaways and Fearless Practices

- Emphasize visible learning over fake teaching.
- Strive for honesty and transparency.
- Solicit feedback on your teaching from colleagues.
- Be demanding AND supportive.
- Use diagnostic assessment well before teaching a unit.
- Most of your assessment should be formative.
- Summative assessments should never surprise you or your students.
- Engage students in self-assessment through setting daily learning targets and tracking improvement over time.
- Give students feedback for how to get better, not advice about what they did wrong.
- Only accept students' best work, consider how you use zeros, and ensure that everyone answers.
- Deal with issues in your classroom.
- Use standardized tests to your advantage.

Open-Ended Case Studies

Select one of the teacher case studies below and answer the associated questions.

- You are a teacher like Laura Fittz, the third-year high school English teacher in a challenging urban high school. You want to continue to grow professionally to enhance your ability to provide academic press and support for your students. Based on your classroom assessments and in the eyes of your evaluators, your students are making progress. However, the standardized tests your students take do not measure growth; instead, they measure their proficiency at one point in time. On those measures, your students are performing well below grade level. Your principal believes you are making more than a year of progress with almost every student in your class and is very supportive of you. How can you use assessment to your advantage in this situation? How can you communicate to your students that they are growing in a way that orients them toward future success? What policies would you change to better support your students in this context?

- You are an experienced teacher in a building filled with solid, collaborative teachers. You have students who do relatively well on state assessments with over 95 percent of students scoring "proficient" or "advanced." Along with specialists and administrators, you focus on those students who are not quite proficient yet hoping to push them into that next level of performance. Sometimes you worry about the lack of attention given to those students at the other end of the spectrum. You wonder if you are demanding enough and providing enough opportunities for them to truly grow. What kinds of things can you do for students who already know much of what the state standards require for your grade level? What role can assessment play? How can you create an environment where you strike the right balance between demand and support for each student?

Reflect

- Think about the press and support 2x2. Where do you most need to grow—in your willingness to consistently demand more of students or in your ability to provide support?

- What percentage of teachers would say they have high expectations for students? What percentage of teachers do you believe actually have high expectations for students?

- How would only accepting students' best work, not giving zeros, and requiring everyone to answer affect your teaching?

- How have you effectively used diagnostic assessment? Formative assessment? Summative assessment?

Risk: 3-2-1 Action Steps

3: Select three related assessments—one diagnostic, one formative, and one student self-assessment and improve them so that they are meaningful indicators of learning.

Possible steps:

- Review the questions on the diagnostic assessment. Do you care about what you will find out from them? Will the questions change the way you will teach the unit?

- Examine the formative assessment. Does the assessment lend itself to advice or feedback?

- Ask your students about the self-assessment. Do they understand what they are a being asked to do? Do they see value in the assessment?

2:   Talk to two colleagues that know you as a teacher.

Possible steps:

- Ask those colleagues about their perception of the level of academic press in your classroom.
- Ask the same colleagues their perception of the support you provide.

1:   Identify one technique that you can use with your students to increase the level of academic press in your teaching.

Possible step:

- Give them fair warning when you give the assignment, and see what happens when you only accept what you perceive to be students' best work on an assignment.

Revise or Reject

After taking a risk, determine what to do next. Was it worthy of revision or rejection?

☐ Reject   ☐ Revise

Write down a few notes about what worked, what did not, and what you might change.

CHAPTER 7

Build Important Relationships

"No significant learning can occur without significant relationship."

— James Comer, Yale University Professor

If you are like me, this quote from Dr. Comer seems like a truism. However, this is not how many schools operate today. We have virtual schools, online academies, enormous comprehensive high schools that function more like factories than learning organizations predicated on relationships. Additionally, we have all learned things on our own, right?

We might be tempted to skip this chapter because we think we get it—good teachers care about students and develop strong relationships in a safe learning environment where growth can occur. We know that relationships with teachers improve student outcomes (Hattie & Yates, 2014). Isn't that about all we need to know?

So, we have at least two questions to address in this chapter if we are going to connect relationships to improved teaching via the novice mindset:

1. Do we really need relationships for significant learning to occur?
2. If we do need relationships for learning, is there anything new to explore?

If you are not like me, you might have actually figured out how to fix something by reading a manual on your own. You might also be adept at Googling any number of things and learning from what you find. Maybe you have participated in a Massive Open Online Course (MOOC) and learned something without forming any relationship with anyone. Maybe you even completed the course unlike the other 96 percent of us who enroll in MOOCs but never complete them (Ho et al., 2014).

The key to Dr. Comer's quotation is the word "significant." What is significant learning? Can we think of anything significant that we have learned that did not involve a relationship? I cannot.

As teachers, we may be most concerned about our relationship with students, but we also know that their relationships with each other could be at least as important as our relationship with them. We also know that some students are in greater

> We also need to remember something that many novice teachers forget: we don't just work with students.

need of relationships with teachers than others, and that, typically, these are the students who we are least likely to engage. We need to find what is fascinating about each student and then be her advocate, mentor, and teacher. To do this, we must be intentional with our students, but we also need to remember something that many novice teachers forget: we don't just work with students. We need to intentionally build relationships with administrators, other teachers, specialists, coaches, paraprofessionals, and secretaries. In addition to relationships inside our buildings, we need to develop relationships beyond our schools.

Fearless Reflection

▶ Before reading the rest of the chapter, rate yourself on your relationships with your students.

- 1 = "I don't know my students' names."
- 10 = "I have deep, meaningful relationships with each student."

| 1 | 2 | 3 | 4 | 5 | 6 | 7 | 8 | 9 | 10 |

What about your relationships with people in your building?

- 1 = "There are other adults who work here?"
- 10 = "I know the birthdays and names of children and grandchildren of every person in my school."

| 1 | 2 | 3 | 4 | 5 | 6 | 7 | 8 | 9 | 10 |

Rate your relationships with people outside of your building including parents, community members, and other educational professionals.

- 1 = "I am a hermit and never leave my classroom."
- 10 = "I could probably be the President of the United States I am so well connected."

| 1 | 2 | 3 | 4 | 5 | 6 | 7 | 8 | 9 | 10 |

FIND WHAT IS FASCINATING

For those of us who have taught a number of years, we know that our most challenging students are often the most interesting. If you ask veteran teachers the names of students that they may have had decades earlier, they may remember the names of super-successful students, but they will definitely remember the names of the students that pushed the boundaries—or just blew right through the boundaries. The great thing about the novice mindset is that we should always be looking to learn about new people, particularly the students who really need us.

> The great thing about the novice mindset is that we should always be looking to learn about new people, particularly the students who really need us.

Record Uniqueness

I discovered a few ways to celebrate the uniqueness of individual students in classes. As all of my students know and as you have likely gathered, I love quotations. One of the ways we celebrated the uniqueness of middle school students was to devote a board to memorable quotations over the course of a year. Most of these were not particularly profound, but were memorable for their unintentional humor (e.g., "Doesn't organic mean plastic?" "I think the skeleton is male because it is bald." "A wind rooster measures wind direction." "If they are sperm whales, are they all guys?"). For my students, the "quote board" became part of our classroom culture and they saw themselves, even if for somewhat embarrassing reasons, celebrated on the board.

Another, more private way, for me to track the uniqueness of my students was through a journal that I have kept for the past nineteen years. There is very little that could be considered profound in that journal, but it helps me to reflect on various students and enjoy who they are as people. Frustration, joy, laughter, and sadness fill the pages of the journal that represents the short time our paths came together, and I had the privilege of walking alongside them. Primarily, the journal is filled with things I appreciated about different students and memorable moments—typically comical things that occurred.

When I was teaching only twenty-five to thirty students a year, those observations became letters that I would write to each student as I brought closure to our relationship to our time together. Honestly, they were more for me than my students, as I needed a time to reflect on their uniqueness, share what I observed, and tell them what I hoped and prayed for them as they moved on from my class.[1] I still do this as a college professor with my students. For our final class together, I give them a book and write the same

---

[1] When I was teaching one hundred middle school students a day, the letters were impossible for me, so they received a DVD with all of the pictures and video projects from their class. I then recorded the quote board and gave them a two to three minute message about what I hoped for them as a class. This was much less personal than the letters but was a way for me to reflect and appreciate my students.

type of note in the front as they move on to other classes or their own class-rooms as teachers.

Give Positive, Specific Recognition—Not Necessarily Praise

This is not a new idea, but some teachers are far better at this than others. Meg Bostrom is a first grade teacher in a suburban district outside of Chicago and is the best teacher I have ever seen do this consistently with every student. A parent described her this way, "Every parent thinks that her child is her favorite student. She knows each child so well and shares her joy with each child." She is one of those teachers that always notices when a student gets a new haircut, is wearing a new pair of Nike socks, or is having a bad day. Every child is a budding mathematician in her classroom. She does have hard conversations with students when they are not meeting her standards, but she can do it in such a way that they know she believes in them. According to colleagues, principals, students, and parents, she does this every day in the ways she interacts with them.

I could never be Meg Bostrom. You may be thinking the same thing. That is fine—we just have to find our own ways of acknowledging students. That is going to look different for middle and high school students. In order to get my students more excited about and working harder at science, at the end of each semester, we organized a "Science Genius Challenge" competition. Students competed as individuals and on teams to determine the "Science Genius" for each class. The winner of this honor received a T-shirt and a nameplate on a plaque that hung outside the lab in the hallway declaring them that semester's Einstein Award winner. Next to that plaque was another plaque for the aptly named Edison Award winner, which was given to the hardest working student in each class each semester. As nerdy as this might sound, my students were quite proud of making the plaque and winning the T-shirts if the number of times they would wear them was any indication.

Whatever we do to recognize students in big or small ways, we need to make it specific. The recognition should be predicated on hard work and growth. It will be most meaningful, if the recognition fits our personalities and the needs of our students.

Spend Time That Is Not Required With Students

One of the best ways to figure out how to recognize and connect with students is to spend time with them outside of the school day. The teacher-student relationship is enhanced, when teachers spend more time with individual students (Pianta & Stuhlman, 2004). Showing up at students' games, performances, shows, or activities communicates that we care about them as human beings and not just as students. This is not news, but we have to prioritize our time because it is a scarce resource. Prioritization may mean attending events for students who most need us to be present.

Sponsoring clubs, coaching, or organizing service projects outside of the school day build relationships that improve the learning environment. Some students flourish outside the classroom in a sport, drama, musical group, or study group. When we are a part of that flourishing, we can capitalize on that success in the classroom. Rafe Esquith and Jaime Escalante took tremendous advantage of this in their classrooms. Escalante's students came in early and on weekends to prepare for the AP Calculus exam. Esquith's students return to his classroom on Saturdays long after they have finished fifth grade for SAT and ACT preparation.

On a more limited scale, I experienced this as a middle school coach. Some members of my boys' basketball team were not the strongest or most motivated students. However, because they loved basketball, I was able to better engage them in science. Our shared bond outside the lab made them much more receptive to what went on inside the lab. It also did not hurt that I could make them run or reduce playing time if they were not performing in other classes.

My girls' basketball team was different. For the most part, they were relatively strong students and good athletes, but they were soccer players playing basketball. One night, I was coaching my fourth game in a row after having taught all day—an "A" and a "B" game for both boys and girls. I was finding it difficult to remain positive because we had not scored in about fifteen minutes of real time. They were playing good defense, running plays perfectly, and missing layup after layup. We lost the game 32–8. While the girls wanted to win, these kinds of losses hardly fazed them and were almost bonding experiences. Due to *my* frustration with losing, I sometimes lost sight of this. As soon as the girls headed home, I called my brother who had been a college basketball coach and asked him what I was doing coaching middle school students. He reminded me, "You are there to build relationships." He was right.

Fearless Reflection

▶ As busy teachers, we must be more strategic about how we will use our time.

• Which students are in greatest need of your time?

• Which activities allow you the most meaningful contact with the most students?

Be Available

One of the most difficult things for most teachers, especially new ones, is feeling like they never have time during the school day. We are rushing to get copies made, preparing materials, giving feedback, figuring out how we are going to manage our classrooms, and trying to keep up with the endless flow of bureaucratic paperwork. Time does seem to slow a bit for us as we gain experience, but teaching is always dominated by the tyranny of the urgent.

Unfortunately, it has been my experience that the time students most need us is almost always the least convenient time for us. We are madly trying to prepare for the next class, get to practice, pick up a child, or get papers graded five minutes before a class is returning, and in walks a student who needs to talk. If we take long enough to look up from our work, we know the telltale signs—moist, downcast eyes, feet shuffling, and a low voice quietly saying our name. No matter what we are doing, we know this is the time we need to listen. We have to be available especially for mercurial, hormone-ravaged middle school students who are more likely to open up through social media than to a trusted adult. Other equally daunting challenges exist for elementary and high school students. Make yourself available because it is likely that the conversation you don't think you have time for represents the very reason why you got into teaching—to help students.

> Time does seem to slow a bit for us as we gain experience, but teaching is always dominated by the tyranny of the urgent.

BE INTENTIONAL

If we are honest with ourselves, we know that there are some students who are tougher to like than others. Most teachers connect well with the relatively mature, well-adjusted students who know how to interact with adults. Those are not the students who need us the most. For students we are struggling to connect with, we need to be intentional.

One strategy for doing this is the "two-by-ten" (Smith & Lambert, 2008). The strategy is fairly straightforward: pick one student who you are struggling to connect with and find a way to talk to him for two minutes every day for ten consecutive days. Find time in the hallway, before school, at lunch, or after school to engage in a conversation for two minutes. The topics of the conversations do not matter. The purpose of these conversations is to get to know the student better and communicate to him that we want to know him as an individual. This can be awkward initially with the student wondering why we are engaging him day after day; however, as we continue to pursue the student and learn about him, these interactions can become more natural. More importantly, the technique works. In a study, disruptive classroom behaviors decreased by 85 percent for students who were the focus of the two-by-ten. I believe there are two reasons for this improvement: 1) The student feels more supported by the teacher, and 2) the teacher better understands the student, how to connect, and what motivates him.

This may be more challenging for high school teachers who might see more than two hundred students a day, but there are opportunities and could become the best twenty-minute investment that we make in a student. The two-by-ten can work at any level with anyone—even colleagues. We just need to be intentional about what we do.

Another strategy that worked well for me as a teacher was greeting students at the door by name each day. Lemov (2010; 2015) describes this as "threshold" and Wong and Wong (2009) have been recommending this practice for years. Again, this does not take a great amount of time, but just requires us to be intentional. There are several obvious benefits to this practice:

1. We communicate to students that each day/period is new. Whatever happened in the hallway or the previous day is behind us.

2. We value them as individuals.

3. We are able to manage the transition into the room and into new work. Students do not straggle into the room as another group leaves. Students do not enter until they are greeted.

4. We should not underestimate the power of a kind word, smile, and the use of students' names. Sometimes students feel that they are not seen or heard. At least for a few seconds, that is not the case.

With my seventh graders, I used this as an opportunity to teach them how to shake hands confidently, a necessary life skill. To avoid hallway congestion, each class waited against the near wall and knew to wait to enter until the previous class had exited. With my fifth graders it could be a handshake, high five, or fist bump. During flu season, it was just a verbal greeting and eye contact. If possible, I would ask a quick question like, "How did your game go last night?" or "Are you feeling better today?" Sometimes it was a simple "Hello" and a name. Students could not enter the room until they returned some type of greeting. After they entered, students engaged in their bell work. Greeting students at the door and the two-by-ten strategy are small ways to be intentional about building relationships with each student.

Ultimately, our relationships with students must be predicated on trust. This is not dependent on personality, but is dependent on students feeling that they are treated fairly, with dignity, and individual respect (Hattie & Yates, 2014). We have to be consistent and intentional in the way we communicate this to students day after day.

When one of my former seventh graders was about to graduate from high school, he committed suicide. I had lost touch with him for several years, but I never would have predicted that life could have gotten so bleak for him.

Even though he was over four years removed from my class, I wondered if there were signs that I missed or things that I could have done to help him find another path. I cannot imagine what his death must have been like for his teachers that had him at the time of his suicide.

Fearless Reflection

- What kinds of things can we do as teachers to make ourselves available for our students?

- Which student is most in need of your attention?

- What can you do to ensure that every student in your class(es) feels that they are seen and known each day?

WE DON'T JUST WORK WITH STUDENTS

Most beginning teachers with whom I work are passionate about developing relationships with students. For many, those relationships are what drew them into teaching. However, we can make a serious mistake if we ignore our other colleagues—administrators, specialists, other teachers, paraprofessionals, secretaries, and custodians. If we believe motivational speaker Jim Rohn when he says, "You are the average of the five people you spend the most time with," then we should be very thoughtful about the people in whom we invest our time beyond our classrooms. I am glad that one of my five people is my wife. She and my kids significantly increase the average of who I am. However, in my school life, who do I spend most of my time with as a teacher? Who are the most influential members of this inner circle of my personal learning network (PLN)?

Office Staff and Custodians

Sometimes those people for me have been office staff and custodians. I realized quickly that the school office staff was vital to my survival as a teacher. Patsy, Mary, Nancy, Betsy, Lorelei, and Patti have taught me, corrected me, caught me before making big mistakes, and covered for me in anything from missing attendance sheets to forgetting important birthdays. The office staff sets the tone for the culture of the school. Often times, they know the

> Teachers can get subs and principals are frequently called out of the building, but the office team is the anchor of the building.

students and families better than anyone else. They also know how to get us extra paper, office supplies, and access to discretionary funds that only they seem to be able to access. Their indispensability is evident whenever they are absent—which never seems to happen. The school does not function nearly as well: announcements do not get made, students get lost, and injured children go unattended. Teachers can get subs and principals are frequently called out of the building, but the office team is the anchor of the building. Not tapping into their expertise is a missed opportunity.

Custodians are also frequently overlooked as significant sources of social capital. As a first-year teacher, I lived in the same apartment complex with Jack, one of our school custodians. He invited me over to his apartment to watch sporting events and stopped by my classroom at the end of each day to check in with me. During those crazy first years of teaching, he was my most regular conversation partner each day. I benefitted from knowing a guy who could fix everything and get extra paper towels when needed. They were still the brown paper towels that pushed water more than absorbed it, but more was better than less. Jack also knew where to find the extra desks, better chairs, and that extra kidney table.

In addition to getting additional resources, I have learned a great deal from the custodians in my building about the culture of the community. When I was teaching in Tennessee, the custodian who cleaned our wing of the school was an African American man from Louisiana. He and I talked almost every day about students, sports, school, and the community. Over the course of four years, I learned as much about being a black man in the South from him than I have from almost anyone else. Our conversations were generally light hearted, but sometimes they would become serious and insightful. On several occasions, he told me, "Jon, that is just the way things are. Things aren't going to change." In most of these instances, I hoped he was wrong, but the insights helped me better understand my students and community.

Developing and maintaining relationships with office staff and custodians is fairly straightforward. These may seem obvious, but we often forget them in our hectic days. Here are five ways to build those relationships:

1. **Say "hello" and use their names:** My first job came at the school where I student taught. One of the reasons the staff and principal hired me was because as a student teacher, I always said "hello" and used everyone's name. Given what you have read about my teaching mistakes, you may be realizing that I needed something other than skill to get hired, and using people's names and greeting them goes a surprisingly long way toward engendering good will.

2. **Treat them as partners in serving our communities**: There is no separation between teachers and others working in the school. We are all on the same team.

3. **Make their jobs easier**: I was terrible at getting my attendance to the office as a beginning teacher. I got better because I knew I was making more work for the office staff. For the custodians, I took two minutes at the end of each day to have my students clean up the floor around them to reduce their work. These efforts did not go unnoticed.

4. **Be thoughtful**: A hand-written note in a staff mailbox goes a long way. The note could be to thank them for their work or to acknowledge important days. Knowing the names of their family members also matters.

5. **Be genuinely interested in their lives**: While it is a distinct advantage to get Super-sorb, the powder absorbent, sprinkled on the vomit in your classroom more quickly, we should develop relationships with others because of who they are and not what they can do for us. Some of the most interesting people with whom we work are the purveyors of Super-sorb.

Mentors

All of us need a mentor in our PLN. Mentors are people we count on and can look to for advice that we can trust.

> We should develop relationships with others because of who they are and not what they can do for us.

These mentors can be administrators or teachers and can be within or outside of our buildings. Two prerequisites for effective mentoring: 1) we need to trust their expertise and 2) they need to know us. This is why some official induction and mentoring programs for teachers are effective and others are not. This is also why some of our best mentors are informal, rather than formal. To illustrate, I had one mentor teacher assigned to me who stopped by my classroom the first week of school to introduce herself and then never stopped by again. She taught in the same building as I did but in another subject area. She was notorious for falling asleep in class when her students were in the room and napping in a supply closet when they were not. Both of the prerequisites for a good mentor were violated.

On the other hand, Priscilla Lane was an informal mentor to me when I first started teaching. I trusted her expertise far more than my own, and we got to know each over the course of our first year working together. Her generosity included providing organized curricular materials, as well as weekly meetings where we discussed upcoming work as a team of teachers. My ideas were valued for the new perspective that they might provide, but largely I was there to learn

> Two prerequisites for effective mentoring: 1) we need to trust their expertise and 2) they need to know us.

that first year. Over time, as my expertise increased and our trust in each other grew, we began to generate new and exciting work together.

As I have moved into the role of mentoring other teachers, I still seek out other mentors. Often, I learn more from the teachers I am supposed to be mentoring than they learn from me. Typically, my learning occurs through reciprocal observation where we switch roles between being the observer and the observed. This can be in person or via digital recording. Our vulnerability and willingness to share cultivates trust that eventually leads to growth.

Fearless Reflection

- Who are the five people you spend the most time with? How do they impact you as a person?

- Who are the five people you spend the most time with professionally? How do they change you as a professional? How do you change them?

- Who is your mentor? Whom do you mentor? What do you do to cultivate trust in those relationships?

CONNECT WITH RESOURCES OUTSIDE YOUR CLASSROOM

Sometimes our growth will lead us out of the classroom to better serve the students inside its walls. At times, we are too busy to recognize the resources that exist outside of our schools, but as we grow in our expertise, we may begin to make space for reaching out beyond the urgency of the moment—not to move into another position, but to better serve our immediate students. Because I have had the opportunity to reach beyond my classroom, I have been exposed to a number of extraordinary teachers who leverage resources far better than I ever have. Justin Minkel and Renee Moore are two of the best examples that I have observed—two people whom I met through my work with the Center for Teaching Quality.

The White House and Home Libraries

Justin Minkel, the 2007 Arkansas Teacher of the Year, is a first and second grade teacher in rural Arkansas at a school where 97 percent of the students live in poverty and 81 percent are English Learners (Arkansas Department of Education, 2014). He is passionate about being a great teacher for his students. Because of this, he is acutely aware of the needs of his students. He loops with his students as a no-cost intervention to better support them in their learning. Looping occurs when a teacher remains with the same group of students for more than one year. There aren't many no-cost interventions, but having students with the same effective teacher for two consecutive years seems like a good one.

Even with his effective instruction over two years, Justin knows that his students need more. He became aware that most of his students had between one and ten books in their homes. He started the "1000 Book Program" to develop home libraries for his twenty-five students. Each of his students received twenty books at each grade level that he taught them. Because of the looping, that totaled one thousand books (forty books times twenty-five students). He describes the success of the initiative:

> "On the DRA [Developmental Reading Assessment], the MAP test [Northwest Evaluation Association Measures of Academic progress], and in one-on-one reading, I saw more growth than I had ever seen in a class. This also had a huge impact on family reading because they were reading to their brothers and sisters. Finally, I had seen a tremendous increase in the love of books."

He scaled the project slowly. The following year, three other teachers at his school tried it. The next year, thirteen teachers implemented the home libraries. The following year, he and a colleague applied for a $100,000 grant to further develop home libraries. Through the CTQ Collaboratory, Twitter, Facebook, and face-to-face conversations, Justin spread his idea in order to garner the votes needed to win the grant, which they did. With the grant money, every teacher in his building is participating, as well as two additional high poverty schools in his district. He points out, "A project that started out impacting twenty-five students will now impact 2,500 students, and the '1000 Books Project' has become the '50,000 Books Project.'"

Justin found ways to partner with Scholastic and won a grant, but he did this largely through engaging colleagues beyond his classroom. He started within his district and then extended beyond Arkansas through CTQ and social media. As he learns from others, his influence also grows. In 2014, he went to the White

> "A project that started out impacting twenty-five students will now impact 2,500 students, and the '1000 Books Project' has become the '50,000 Books Project.'"

House to discuss education issues with President Obama and three other teachers over lunch. He is certainly reaching beyond his classroom.

Rejecting the "Culture of Poverty"

Renee Moore has been an English teacher in the Mississippi Delta for over twenty-five years. I have had the opportunity to learn from her on several occasions. She is the consummate teacher in the way she talks about teaching and learning. For her, teaching has always been about her students and what they do. She has been the Mississippi Teacher of the Year, a Milken Educator, has National Board Certification, and was the first practicing teacher to sit on the board of directors of the Carnegie Foundation; but I did not learn this from her. When she talks, it is about her students, learning, and faith. She and her husband have served their community through the church where he is a pastor and her work as a teacher. They are significant connectors in the dense social fabric of their community.

To illustrate Renee's way of communicating, here is an excerpt of one of her emails to a student of mine who was going to teach in the Mississippi Delta. This was her introduction from Renee:

> Welcome to Mississippi. I have taught here in the Mississippi Delta region for nearly 25 years, most of that at the high school level. I have always taught in schools that were 98–100 percent free and reduced lunch—high poverty, high-needs schools. I do not believe in the so-called "culture of poverty." Poverty is an enforced condition in which people are forced to survive. Here in the Delta, I have taught some of the finest students you can imagine, and I have worked with some of the greatest teachers and administrators anywhere.

This introduction to her context is powerful. She brings this type of fearless honesty to all of her work and her students. Her exposure to the wider education system has benefitted her students, but more importantly, the system's exposure to her has benefited all of those that work in education. Renee is not afraid to go public with her teaching (Hatch et al., 2005), and her generosity with colleagues represents the type of leadership that improves the entire profession.

Teachers like Justin and Renee make us proud to be teachers. They know what it means to build relationships with students and colleagues both within and beyond the classroom. Because of that they have greater influence and their passion for teaching grows. They have recognized what matters in their work and remain focused on their students; however, they continue to seek out new challenges in support of that focus, pushing into new areas of growth. They are expert novices.

By now, you should know that I won't be asking you to be like them. We all must find our own way to meet the needs of our students. In the final chapter, we will explore how you can become an expert novice if you are just starting out in teaching or you are an experienced teacher. Maybe your inner novice is feeling a bit overwhelmed or has been buried under an avalanche of paperwork, bureaucracy, and other soul-deadening minutia. Wherever you are on the career continuum, this final chapter will provide you a way forward.

Key Takeaways and Fearless Practices

- Significant learning requires significant relationships.
- Find what is fascinating and unique about each student and record it.
- Think about closure as the year comes to an end.
- Give positive, specific recognition and less general praise.
- Spend time with students outside of the time you have them in class—recess, events, games, clubs, etc.
- Do not let the tyranny of the urgent keep you from being available to your students. They rarely need you when it is convenient.
- Try the two-by-ten.
- Think about how you will create a threshold for your classroom. Teaching students how to shake hands is a valuable life skill.
- Remember to intentionally connect with everyone who works in your building.
- Find a mentor and be a mentor. Choose wisely—"you are the average of the five people you spend the most time with."
- Connect with resources outside your classroom. There are amazing teachers doing amazing things.

Open-Ended Case Studies

Select one of the teacher case studies below and answer the associated questions.

- Grace is a student teacher who has an excellent relationship with her students and her cooperating teacher. However, she is struggling to connect with other teachers and staff in the building. Everyone seems friendly but busy. She is unsure of what she should do as a student teacher who will only be in the building for a semester. What steps could Grace take to connect with other teachers and staff? What difference does her context make (i.e., Does it matter if it is an elementary, middle, or high school?)? Beyond seeking advice from her cooperating teacher, how could Grace determine what is appropriate to do to engage others as colleagues?
- In twelve years of teaching, you have never had such a challenging class. You had heard for years that this class was coming and was the worst class in school history. You tried not to believe it, but you are losing your resolve to remain positive. There are two boys in particular who seem intent on wrestling control of your class from you.

What is one way you could attempt to build relationships with these two boys? What are the barriers to you making this attempt? What is difficult for you personally as you make efforts to build relationships with boys who are openly disrespectful and seem to despise you?

Reflect

- As a student, what was the most significant relationship you had with a teacher? What is the most significant learning that occurred because of this relationship?

- How can you find and celebrate what is fascinating about your students?

- What is one way you can communicate to your students that you are available to listen? In the same way, what members of your school community do you need to build relationships with? How will you go about doing this?

- How can you extend your relationships beyond your school to continue to grow?

Risk: 3-2-1 Action Steps

3: Identify three students in your class(es) with whom you need to deepen your relationship.

Possible steps:

- Try the two-by-ten strategy one student at a time. The two-by-ten is difficult even when you only target one student at a time.

- Connect with the student by spending some time outside of the school day—go to a performance, game, or do a home visit.

- Do a home visit.

2: Identify two members of your school community with whom you need to develop a relationship.

Possible steps:

- Put a note in the person's mailbox letting them know you appreciate something that he or she does.

- Ask a question about something unrelated to school and really listen.

1: Identify one person or group beyond your building with whom you need to develop a relationship.

Possible steps:

- Join the CTQ Collaboratory.
- Follow someone you respect on Twitter.

Revise or Reject

After taking a risk, determine what to do next. Was it worthy of revision or rejection?

☐ Reject   ☐ Revise

Write down a few notes about what worked, what did not, and what you might change.

PART III
Expert Novices

CHAPTER 8

Become an Expert Novice

"A medical study showed that if heart doctors tell their seriously at-risk heart patients they will literally die if they do not make changes to their personal lives—diet, exercise, smoking—still only one in seven is actually able to make changes."

Immunity to Change (Kegan & Lahey, 2009, p. 1)

We have an immunity to change. This mental "immune system" is vital for our self-preservation. We all have highly developed systems that protect us from external pressures that threaten us personally and professionally (See Kegan & Lahey, 2009 for a much deeper explanation). For teachers, these can be highly complex systems that have been refined over years as students and as educators. Refined by poor teaching models, teaching practices that did not work for us, endless initiatives that will revolutionize teaching, incessant school reform, constant administrator churn, negative colleagues, or self-doubt. Our professional immune system fights off the things that we fear or threaten who we are as teachers.

So, an immune system is a good thing, right? Yes, except for when it kills six out of seven at-risk heart patients . . . or six out of seven teaching careers. With the heart patients, lack of change is not due to a lack of desire. We are probably safe to assume that they want to live. Sometimes we do not change because we apply technical solutions to adaptive challenges—challenges that can only be overcome by transforming our mindset (Heifetz, 1998 in Kegan & Lahey, 2009). For the heart patient, that might mean trying to stop smoking cold turkey without addressing the underlying reason why she smokes. For the person who is trying to lose weight, this might be going on a diet without addressing the underlying reason why he overeats. What might be needed is a significant change in who we are to make a major shift in what we do. That is why this book cannot be reduced to a series of technical solutions or practices. What is required is a mindset and process—an orientation toward teaching, learning, and ourselves.

> Often times, this is the problem with our education system. We apply technical solutions to adaptive challenges that really require a complete reorientation of how we think about school.

Often times, this is the problem with our education system. We apply simplistic technical solutions to adaptive challenges that really require a complete reorientation of how we think about school. The technical solutions (e.g., Positive Behavior Intervention Supports, Response to Intervention, differentiation, scripted curriculum, etc.) are neither good nor bad. They are just the technical answers to complex challenges. Kegan and Lahey (2009), point out that the average person who loses ten pounds eventually gains 107 percent of that weight back. In education, this is the equivalent of a simplistic, poorly implemented solution to an adaptive challenge that may have some initial traction but ultimately leads to disillusionment. Teachers may feel they are worse off than they were before the initiative. The dieter's or the teacher's immune system kicks into overdrive. The dieter and the teacher become that much more cynical and pessimistic about the likelihood of positive change.

According to a recent study of three large school districts in the United States, they spend $18,000 per teacher annually on their development (The New Teacher Project, 2015). They actually found that this had no impact on their effectiveness. Is this because teachers can't improve or because the development in question might have focused on technical solutions to adaptive challenges?

Sometimes when we refuse to change it is out of fear that we will lose who we are. Changes that force teachers to lose who they are (e.g., scripted curriculum, top-down management, tone-deaf policies, etc.) should stimulate our teacher immune system. But what about those changes that could help us improve?

For good or bad, we are who we are, right?

We can't really get back to a mindset where we can be honest, vulnerable, and fearless about our weaknesses, can we?

> Our work begins when we get to the end of this chapter.

I know we can change. Our profession and our students need us to grow. This chapter is full of examples of our colleagues who have become expert novices. Real teachers across the country are doing this hard work. Our work begins when we get to the end of this chapter. We will complete maps to launch the next stage of our growth as expert novices. Although seemingly paradoxical expert novices are humble learners who continue to seek opportunities to reflect, risk, and grow with others. We do this by

- getting better in our classrooms,
- getting better in others' classrooms,

- getting better beyond the classroom, and
- becoming expert novices by seeking opportunities.

GETTING BETTER IN OUR CLASSROOMS

As we have already established, novices grow when they become more aware of how their students are learning. As a result, their confidence about what they are teaching grows. As this happens, we move outside of our own heads and into the heads of our students—an infinitely interesting place to develop our novice expertise about them. We are no longer teaching math, science, reading, or music, we are teaching individuals. This makes growth and change much easier because teaching is no longer about us.

Assessment Data and Beyond

Assessment data is a snapshot of where students are with regard to particular skills. Morgan McClymonds is a third-year teacher and a master with standardized assessment data. Instead of being intimidated by the Northwest Evaluation Association Measures of Academic Progress (MAP) test data, Morgan has embraced it with her first graders. They take the computer adaptive assessment three times a year in reading and math. She describes what she does with the data.

> "After the December test, I meet with each student and parents if they are able to show them their test results. We discuss their growth and I show them the goals I've made. They each have a chance to make their own goals as well—things like tying shoes, riding a two-wheel bike, or learning more about giraffes. I tape the learning goals to students' desk. As they move through the school year, we check off goals that they have met. This year every student met every goal! In math, students grew an average of 26.4 points. In reading, students grew an average of 22.6 points. The national norm for first grade is 16 points for both math and reading. Most of the time I have to develop multiple units in math because students' math scores show that about a third of the class already knows the skills."

We probably all know schools where teachers use data with their students. But this was Morgan's idea—not a mandate from her principal. Before dismissing Morgan as a teacher who only cares about data, here are a few other snapshots of her classroom that are equally, if not more, valuable in her own words:

- "We had a *Henry and Mudge* Valentine's Day Dance. I taught my students how to waltz to "The Blue Danube." They were asking each other to waltz at recess. I got an email from a parent saying that her daughter 'just waltzed with her grandpa.'"

FIGURE 8.1 Morgan's Waltzing Students

- "A Chinese American friend and I exposed my almost entirely African American class to Chinatown's Moon Festival in Chicago. My friend brought red bean cakes for all the students to eat. The middle school students would not touch them, but every one of my first graders tried them."

- "We performed a play with twenty-four speaking parts, 'The Friendliest Fish and the Sea,' from *Big Al* by Andrew Clements. We went to the Shed Aquarium to see each student's character. We had costumes including a transparent umbrella with LED lights for a jellyfish. The sea stars had to walk like sea stars, and the sea anemones had crazy hats. We invited the parents to an evening performance and made seventy-five programs. Before the doors were even supposed to open, the programs were gone, the parking lot was full, and the principal had to make more programs. That night, two hundred family members showed up for the performance."

This is not a teacher who believes school is all about test scores. This is a teacher who knows who she is, will reflect, risk, and grow. She is a teacher with a novice mindset who is becoming an expert novice.

Classroom Innovation

Sometimes we need to find the right spot to get better in our own classrooms. Marcey Wennlund, the first-year teacher from the first chapter who was getting feedback on how many seconds of sharing should occur and how many claps to provide on a weekly if not daily basis, moved out of state to a new teaching position. She took a pay cut and is moving over one thousand miles to enter a classroom where she hopes she can grow as a teacher. She says, "I am changing grade levels to go to a new school for less pay,

FIGURE 8.2 Two "Rainbow Fish"

fewer resources, less technology, similar students, for more autonomy in my literacy block."

Andrew Berndt is a brilliant math teacher. He completed his student teaching in Quito, Ecuador and then took a teaching job in Macon, Georgia. He had a successful first year of teaching and connected with students and their families partially by tapping into his quirky love for mathematics. For example, he would arrive at athletic events and sit in the stands raising posters of support in the form of mathematical equations.

After his first year, he determined that his students would learn more if he flipped his classroom. He went online and figured out presentation software and then began recording demonstration problems and explanations. His first efforts were too long (online tutorials should be no longer than the intended grade level—e.g., tenth graders will watch about ten minutes) and not very interesting. At the end of the year, he informally surveyed his students and parents and found that many of them did not really like the

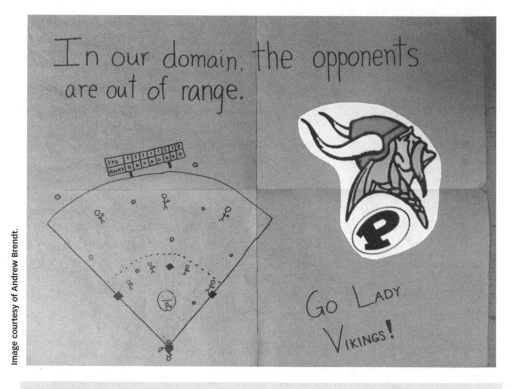

FIGURE 8.3 One of Andrew's Softball Signs

Image courtesy of Andrew Brendt.

flipped lessons. Unlike what most of us might have done, he did not give up on the idea. He continues to refine the lessons, and parents and students are slowly coming around. Even if they do not entirely come to see the benefit, he says, "I am going to keep doing it because I know from my assessments that my students are learning more math, more deeply." Andrew has found a place where he can innovate for the benefit of his students. Hopefully, Marcey will as well.

GETTING BETTER IN OTHERS' CLASSROOMS

If Marcey, Andrew, or you get better in your own classroom, that benefits the particular students in those classrooms, but what if we want to improve more than just our own classrooms? How do we "go public" with our teaching in a way that makes others around us better as others have suggested is vital to the improvement of the education system (Berry, 2010; Berry et al., 2013; Hatch et al., 2005)?

> How do we "go public" with our teaching in a way that makes others around us better?

First, we cannot be fearful. Renee Moore, the impactful Mississippi teacher from the last chapter, describes it this way, "I am a woman of faith; I don't believe in fear, period" (Berry et al., 2013, p. 71).

Renee also derives strength from collaboration, belief in the work she is doing, and from the resilience of her students. Wherever we derive our courage, we need this to lead well in others' classrooms.

Second, we must be vulnerable and open to feedback. If we want to help others get better, then we must be transparent with our practice and seek feedback from colleagues. Japanese lesson study is predicated on this type of vulnerable collaboration where teachers design lessons, teach them, observe one another teaching the same lesson, and then reflect together. This is not the culture in most U.S. schools, but this is a culture that we can create by inviting others into our practice.

Third, we need time and opportunity. We need to be in each other's classrooms for reciprocal observation. This can be done through video or even better through in-person visits or coteaching. Observations benefit both the observed and the observer. In a recent survey of State Teachers of the Year, the highest ranked experience for developing their own effectiveness as teacher leaders was "formal coaching or mentoring colleagues to improve their instructional practice" (Behrstock-Sherratt, Bassett, Olson, & Jacques, 2014, p. 21). This may require structural changes to the school day, but until this happens, we will be unlikely to get better together.

Some schools are making these structural changes to create time and opportunity. One example is the TAP System.

Basics of the TAP System

- "Master" teachers receive 80 percent release time from their classrooms (roughly one for every fifteen teachers).

- "Mentor" teachers receive 20 percent release time from their classrooms (roughly one for every eight teachers).

- Weekly seventy-five minute job-embedded professional development led by the master or mentor teacher with small groups of teachers.

  o Master or mentor presents a strategy.
  o The following week, that strategy is implemented or cotaught with students.
  o The next meeting, teachers bring work from students with high, middle, and low examples.
  o The strategy is revised or a new strategy based on needs identified in student work is introduced.

- Increased compensation based on additional work and student learning outcomes.

Having observed these master and mentor teachers in classrooms and the weekly team meetings at schools implementing the TAP System, I am convinced that the way to improve teaching is to observe others, coteach, and honestly evaluate student work. Notice the similarities between the structure of the TAP System and Japanese lesson study. Most teachers in these schools say they appreciate the additional compensation, but the primary benefit they cite is the ability to get better together (Eckert, 2010, 2013).

Two Novice Examples

Tamara Hoey and Kate Cauhorn are teachers in Chicago. Tamara teaches first graders at LEARN Charter School. Kate teaches middle school students at UNO Esmeralda Santiago Charter School. They have been teaching for four and five years respectively. They are no longer novices, but they are gaining expertise by maintaining novice mindsets. Tamara describes the sweet spot she is in right now for developing as a teacher leader.

> I now have trust and credibility. I did not have that my first two years. Now I am in a master's program in teacher leadership at Northwestern University. I am really interested in the use of video for personal learning. I think it can revolutionize practice when we can reflect on what teachers are saying and doing. Next year, I want to do video clubs with teachers at our schools.

Tamara is growing as a teacher by taking risks as a leader. Eventually she hopes to be able to take on new roles "without having to go into administration."

She would like to be an academic interventionist, a coach, or have a flexible role that would allow her to stay or rotate back into the classroom regularly. These new opportunities will allow her to become an expert novice.

Kate is already leading in her school both formally and informally. She was the teacher of the year in her school this year and is using the credibility she has to help make structural changes to her school. More importantly, she is extending leadership to other teachers. She recounted a conversation with a colleague:

"Don't you think you would be a much better teacher if you could just teach math?"

When the teacher answered affirmatively, she said, "Why don't you tell the administration? I have done that, and it worked well for me."

Additionally, Kate sees a need for coteaching to occur and improvements in Response to Intervention (RtI). She is working with teachers and administrators to try to bring about these changes. She says, "I have freedom and trust from my boss, so I am able to ask for new schedules or restructured meetings. We have shared responsibility." Like Tamara, she is interested in hybrid roles that will allow her to remain in the classroom, but continue to grow beyond the classroom.

Like any good teacher who is collaborating with others, Kate sees ways in which the school can improve. Each week, all of the teachers attend thirty-minute RtI meetings. She bluntly states, "Teachers hate these meetings. We need specialists to push in to our classrooms, and we need to coteach." Kate is learning how to extend her influence beyond the walls of her classroom with her leadership, but it is challenging. "We have pushback to change because people don't want to be first-year teachers again as we change. I want to encourage teachers to try new things." Kate has encapsulated the challenge of having a novice mindset when that mindset is not shared. Tamara could encounter the same challenge with video for personal learning if she tries to engage others in this growth process. How do they navigate these challenges?

An Expert With a Novice Mindset

Possibly a good place to look is fifteen years ahead of Tamara and Kate. They might become the next Joan Dabrowski. Outside of Boston, Baltimore, or literacy expert circles, people may not have heard of Joan. However, she has been getting better in other people's classrooms for years. She started her career as one of the first Teach For America corps members in an urban classroom in Houston. Having been a music performance major in college without an education degree, she learned a great deal from her students in those first few years. Those students won her heart and mind for urban education. She has taught in Houston, Detroit, and Boston and remains a passionate educator; however, she no longer has her own classroom. She has hundreds of classrooms along the East Coast.

I met Joan in our doctoral classes at Vanderbilt University. At the time, she was the mother of two young children, married to an elementary school principal, was a district literacy coach for the Cambridge Public Schools, and commuting eighteen weekends a year to class—from Boston to Nashville where Vanderbilt is located. She always made me feel better about my workload when I saw her. I share her "life load" to demonstrate the challenges that Kate and Tamara may face as they expand their influence beyond their immediate classrooms.

Currently, Joan is a consultant supporting literacy instruction in school districts and in nonprofit organizations. She spends many days each year visiting and working in classrooms along the East Coast. Joan is committed to improving the literacy skills of urban students—this has been her life's work. Her desire to spread her influence has taken her out of her own classroom and into others'. The workload she has maintained at points in her career would have been too much for many teachers. This is the problem with the way teachers' work is currently designed. For Joan and for us to spread our expertise and grow with other colleagues, we may have to leave our own classrooms behind, spread ourselves really thin, and then deal with other teachers who no longer think we are "real teachers." There is urgency in our own classrooms when we teach students every day that makes this critique sting for those of us who teach in others' classrooms. However, telling novice teacher leaders like Kate and Tamara that Joan is no longer a "real teacher" is counterproductive.

> We need more teacher leaders—more who can come into our classrooms, stay in their own if possible, and continue to take risks and grow.

Joan is exactly the kind of leader we want in others' classrooms. She has deep expertise in literacy, is constantly reading the latest research, coteaches on a regular basis, and listens and sees through her classroom teaching filter. Her filter gives her great respect for teachers and understanding for the challenges we face. To accommodate the needs of her family and her needs as an individual, Joan has become a consultant, but she will maintain credibility as a teacher because she understands that there is a difference between what she does now and what she did twenty years ago. That said, she has gained and shared a tremendous amount of expertise and experience that she could not have attained if she had stayed in her classroom full time. She learns from teachers every day. Now she shares that with us in books, guides, and coaching. We need more teacher leaders—more who can come into our classrooms, stay in their own if possible, and continue to take risks and grow.

GETTING BETTER BEYOND THE CLASSROOM

To maintain a novice mindset and continue to grow in expertise, teachers need new opportunities. The education system needs what those teachers

► Are you willing to grow with other teachers in their classrooms?

- 1 = "I do not even like talking to other teachers."
- 10 = "I do Japanese lesson study on Saturday nights with my teacher friends."

1	2	3	4	5	6	7	8	9	10

How frequently do you grow with others by going public with your practice or seeing others teach?

- 1 = "My principal locks me in my room daily."
- 10 = "I am able to get in other teachers' classrooms on a daily basis."

1	2	3	4	5	6	7	8	9	10

What barriers are inhibiting you from sharing expertise with other teachers?

- Self?
- Others?
- Resources?

will produce in those new opportunities. For too long, we have viewed teaching as an isolated experience where teachers will go into a classroom and emerge forty years later at retirement. This is not particularly appealing to young teachers, nor is it best for the profession. In the epilogue to *The Teacher Wars*, a very readable history of the teaching profession in the U.S., Dana Goldstein prescribes several solutions to the problems that ail our system. She recommends, "Keep teaching interesting." She writes:

> A set of job responsibilities that remains stagnant over the course of five, ten, or twenty years can leave teachers feeling burned out and bored and drives some high performers uninterested in becoming administrators out of the profession. If we expect ambitious, intellectually engaged people to become teachers and remain in our public schools, we must offer them a career path that is exciting and varied over the long term, and which includes opportunities to lead adults, not just children. (2014, pp. 65–66)

I hear versions of this from preservice to veteran teachers as well as from college students who do not choose teaching. However, some places are beginning to understand the need for these varied career paths. Goldstein describes Singapore where after three years, teachers are expected to pursue a leadership path in curriculum writing, school administration, or mentoring. In Baltimore and many other districts across the U.S., districts are experimenting with hybrid roles for teachers so that they can lead without leaving their classrooms (Berry et al., 2013). To more strategically use compensation in these instances, there could be value in rewarding effective teachers who take on responsibility to help other teachers improve student learning (Goldstein, 2014).

These opportunities for those expert novices who want to grow should extend beyond the school and district. We need the expertise of teacher leaders in state and federal policy creation, and teachers need to grow in these areas through additional opportunities. What follows are brief examples of what this might look like based on examples that are already occurring.

Teachers and Policy

Most of us roll our eyes when we talk about state and federal policy. We think of bureaucrats and politicians sitting in state capitals and Washington, DC, far removed from students and reality, crafting uninformed policies that make our lives more difficult. Are you rolling your eyes now? While it still remains challenging to inform policymaking, some teachers are influencing policies through collaboration at the state and federal levels. Organizations like the Center for Teaching Quality, Hope Street Group, and Teach Plus are elevating teachers into policy development (Pennington, 2013).

One high school English teacher, Jocelyn Pickford, was on leave from her classroom for a prestigious White House Fellowship in 2007 when she attended a panel discussion with the U.S. Secretary of Education, Margaret Spellings. After hearing much of the discussion center around teachers and the teaching profession, she was moved to speak up during the question and answer session, introducing herself and then saying:

> I am a teacher, but I am not here because I am a teacher. I am here because I am also a White House Fellow. While I'm extremely proud of my Fellowship, I'm equally proud of my role as a teacher—and I would not have been here if I was teaching full time. My question is: why are we having these conversations without teachers?

> Why are we having these conversations without teachers?

This question prompted Secretary Spellings to send Jocelyn a hand-written note acknowledging the issue—and to eventually hire her to bring the idea to reality at the U.S. Department of Education. Jocelyn points out, "Secretary Spellings had been thinking about a formal way to recognize and engage teachers, and my question aligned well with her desire." Over the next several months, the Teaching Ambassador Fellowship was born. With the help of Gillian Cohen-Boyer,[1] Jocelyn brought five teachers to the Department full time and connected twenty teachers who remained in their classrooms and collaborated with federal policymakers part-time as the first cohort of the Teaching Ambassador Fellows in 2008. After the presidential election, Jocelyn took her teaching perspective and policy skills to new opportunities in education. She now works with the New Jersey Department of Education, where she has been integral in the creation of a state initiative to recognize outstanding teachers and empower them to take on leadership roles in their schools and districts—and to provide vital feedback to the State Department.[2] Her legacy as an advocate for increasing teachers' influence on policy continues to grow at the U.S. Department of Education as well. Eight cohorts of Fellows have worked with the Department since the Fellowship began.

Two of those Fellows are teachers Edit Khachatryan and Jasmine Ulmer, from California and Florida respectively. Edit left the classroom to serve as a Fellow in Washington, DC, and Jasmine remained in her classroom and worked with the Department part-time. They are both forceful advocates for students and are quick to question and redirect policymakers who lose sight of students. Their hearts are still in the classroom with students, but both finished the Fellowship and enrolled in doctoral programs at Stanford University and the University of Florida. They have enhanced their abilities to advocate for students by developing research agendas in support of teacher leadership and policies that will benefit all students. They were novices in the policy and research world, but have been expert teachers. This is a powerful and necessary combination.

Steven Hicks is an early childhood teacher from Los Angeles. Like Edit, he came to the U.S. Department of Education as a Fellow. When he came, he had two dreams:

> They were novices in the policy and research world, but have been expert teachers. This is a powerful and necessary combination.

1. He would get on Oprah.
2. The U.S. Department of Education would create an Office of Early Learning.

Steven's dream of getting on Oprah has not been realized, but there is now an Office of Early Learning. He has been at the U.S. Department of Education for seven years, and has worked tirelessly to bring this dream to fruition,

---

[1] Gillian still leads the Fellowship and is one of the over four thousand career employees at the Department. Even at this size, the U.S. Department of Education remains the smallest of the fifteen cabinet-level departments in the executive branch of the federal government. The Fellowship now includes a Principal Ambassador Fellowship, and the goals remain essentially the same.

[2] The New Jersey Achievement Coaches program was launched in February 2015 and has involved over 150 educators to date.

and continues to work to ensure its impact. His students continue to inform his work and advocacy. After seven years in Washington, he is now a policy expert. Coupled with his teaching expertise, he is a formidable advocate who is constantly searching for new opportunities to grow.

Preparing Teachers to Influence Policy

In the spring of her freshman year, Abby Canfield approached me about an independent study on education policy. Just weeks before, Brad Jupp, a Senior Program Advisor to the U.S. Secretary of Education, had reached out to me to see if I had a student interested in conducting research on tenure law. A perfect match was made. Abby spent her summer in law libraries researching the history of Illinois tenure law. She was completely engrossed. That fall, she had several research calls in my office with Brad where they discussed what she had found. I listened in amazement as they discussed the esoteric details of the legislative and statutory history of tenure law in Illinois. The following summer, Abby landed an internship at the U.S. Department of Education. Admittedly, this is not the dream of most teachers, but I am convinced this will inform Abby's teaching and leadership as she moves into the classroom and becomes an expert novice in practice and policy.

Teacher-Powered Schools

Even more than influencing policy, some of us have imagined what schools might be like if they were teacher-led or teacher-powered. Everyone would teach students every day with release time for requisite leadership and administrative work. Administrators would lead in very different ways and their responsibilities would be distributed amongst teachers at these schools. I had no idea these schools existed until I met Lori Nazareno.

Lori is one of the most quietly forceful advocates for teachers that I have met. She kind of intimidates me, even when she isn't talking, which is most of the time. She is the cofounder of the Math and Science Leadership Academy in Denver. This is a school without administrators. Along with others, Lori took on leadership responsibilities while teaching on a regular basis. She had credibility as a teacher and the grounding of being with students regularly. Now she leads the Center for Teaching Quality's work around teacher-powered initiatives that advocate and support teachers' efforts to solve problems and carve out autonomy in the service of their students.

Lori is a learner. She always has new books that she can recommend and new ideas to share because she listens and observes. Then she acts. She is realistic about the challenges teachers face, but she trusts other teachers. "I know I have the ability to see things and how they can be different. One of my strengths is leading teachers, many of whom have been socialized to work in isolation, to move in the same direction" (Berry et al., 2013, p. 116).

All of the opportunities described above require a change in the education system particularly as it relates to the design of the work of teaching and administration—particularly the associated leadership work (Crowther, Ferguson, & Hann, 2009; Eckert & Smylie, 2014; Murphy, 2005). We have entered an era of education where we cannot fully imagine the contours of the classroom ten years from now. In some respects, we will all be novices in multiple aspects of what might lie ahead. If we have gotten this far in the book together, we know that this is not something to be feared. We welcome change and the opportunity to adapt.

Fearless Reflection

▶ How willing are you to lead beyond the classroom?

- 1 = "Close the door, and leave me alone."
- 10 = "Sign me up for U.S. Secretary of Education."

| 1 | 2 | 3 | 4 | 5 | 6 | 7 | 8 | 9 | 10 |

What skills, knowledge, and experiences do you have that could benefit our profession and increase your scope of influence?

How would you rate your opportunities to lead beyond the classroom?
- 1 = "My principal said I could do bus duty."
- 10 = "I have been asked to become the superintendent for our district."

| 1 | 2 | 3 | 4 | 5 | 6 | 7 | 8 | 9 | 10 |

What opportunities do you have to increase your influence beyond the classroom?

BECOMING EXPERT NOVICES

To become expert novices, we cannot lose our novice selves. To do this, we must position ourselves as learners, stretch beyond what is comfortable, and constantly seek new challenges. All of this is best done with others.

Position Yourself as a Learner

Putting ourselves in positions where we have to ask for help is uncomfortable, but it is the easiest way to create teachable moments. Some teachers are extremely comfortable in their classrooms and this can be fine, but there may be some ways that they could extend themselves that would benefit more teachers and more students. There is also something invigorating about taking on a new challenge where we are not sure if we will actually be able to succeed.

Brad Jupp, the Senior Program Advisor from the U.S. Department of Education who worked with Abby on tenure law, is an example of someone who positions himself as a learner. A nineteen-year teaching veteran when he came to the Department, he recognized the value of making relationships with key people. He purposely sought out teachers in the Department and collected information from them on the people he needed to know. He has been the point person on teacher initiatives over the last six years and has learned a great deal. When the current administration comes to an end, he plans to go back into a middle school English classroom to teach. He is excited to test the effectiveness of some of the initiatives he has led from the Department. He knows there will be a learning curve after having been removed from the classroom for eight years, but he relishes the opportunity to grow.

Barnett Berry, the founder of the Center for Teaching Quality, loves his role because he is able to learn from amazing teachers. When he introduces himself to teachers, he always says, "It is a privilege to work with you. You are far better teachers than I ever was. Thank you for your work in the profession that makes all others possible." When we sincerely believe that we can learn from and grow with others, we increase the likelihood of becoming expert novices because we have humbly positioned ourselves in a stance that is open to growth. Brad and Barnett are in positions where many people look to them as the people that should have all of the answers, but they both spend time listening instead of always talking, and you can see that the ideas of others energize them. When was the last time we were energized by someone else's ideas?

When was the last time we were energized by someone else's ideas?

Stretch

Morgan McClymonds, the first-grade teacher highlighted earlier, is one of the biggest risk takers I know. She has worked in an orphanage in Guatemala City where she contracted dengue fever (known as "bone crushing fever" for the pain it causes) taught in Ecuador and the south side of Chicago, and is always applying for opportunities like "Teacher at Sea" where teachers live on a ship in Antarctica. Between her third and fourth years of teaching, she got the opportunity to live in Denali National Park in Alaska for six weeks to design curriculum for elementary school teachers about dinosaurs in Denali. However, she was uncertain about whether to make this stretch. She would be missing out on family commitments, relationships, relaxation, and Chicago—one of the greatest cities in the world in the summer.

Often when we are faced with opportunities to stretch ourselves, there are competing good options. Morgan almost didn't go to Denali. In the end, however, she decided to stretch. All summer she posted blogs and answered questions from her students. She posted videos and pictures of wolves, caribou, moose, grizzly bears, and the sled dog that she adopted and cared for over the summer. The richness of her experience will not only change her as a teacher, it will change her as a person. Because she is sharing the experience with her first graders, she is also opening a part of the world to them that they might never have considered. She is modeling adventurous risk taking that could have ripple effects for years to come.

The Four Rs process is equal parts reflection and risk taking. In *Immunity to Change*, Kegan and Lahey (2009) describe why it is so hard for us to take some risks. We are afraid of what those risks might cost us—credibility, respect, self-worth, or our identity. However, taking risks is the only way to truly develop our novice mindset in ways that will allow us to grow. We need to take chances that stretch us for our professional growth and as models for our students. One of the best ways we can do this is by cultivating relationships inside and outside of the classroom as described in Chapter 7. We cannot expect our students to take risks if we are unwilling to lead by example.

At the end of *Better*, Dr. Atul Gawande gives a final piece of advice about the need for change. He writes,

> Look for the opportunity to change. I am not saying you should embrace every new trend that comes along. But be willing to recognize the inadequacies in what you do and to seek out solutions. As successful as medicine [insert "teaching" for "medicine"] is, it remains replete with uncertainties and failures. This is what makes it human, at times painful, and also so worthwhile. (2007, p. 257)

Gawande does include an important caveat that most educators will resonate with, don't "embrace every new trend that comes along." This is particularly good advice for administrators and policymakers. So often these are technical solutions to adaptive challenges. These shortsighted technical solutions breed cynicism in us as teachers.

> Meaningful change that serves our students better is often what makes teaching so worthwhile because the change is born of the recognition of our inadequacies.

Please note that this book is not meant to be a set of technical solutions to the challenges of teaching. Meaningful change that serves our students better is often what makes teaching so worthwhile because the change is born of the recognition of our inadequacies. This makes our weaknesses rich opportunities for growth.

▶ How effective are you at being a learner?

- 1 = "Students just need to learn everything I know."

- 10 = "I love to teach because I love to learn. I learn everyday from students and colleagues."

1	2	3	4	5	6	7	8	9	10

What opportunities do you have to stretch yourself professionally?

What, if anything, inhibits your ability to change? Your colleagues' ability to change?

What is an example of a technical solution that has been applied to an adaptive challenge? What might have been an adaptive solution?

THE EXPERT NOVICE OPPORTUNITY

So far, this chapter has included numerous examples of teachers who are expert novices. We may already recognize ourselves in many of these examples. Or maybe we are defensively shutting down and thinking to ourselves, "These people have no lives, work all the time, and have opportunities I will never have." I hope we are in the former mindset and not getting defensive—that is the enemy of the novice mindset. As an encouragement about being a novice and stepping forward to take on new challenges in education, how many days of teaching experience have the last two U.S. Secretaries of Education had? Their combined teaching experience equals a grand total of zero days. This is not meant to disparage either Arne Duncan or Margaret Spellings. They are both well-meaning, intelligent human beings who care about students and understand policymaking. But my point is, what is keeping you from being a future Secretary of Education? If you are like me, it is probably a lack of desire because it is a difficult and thankless job that is miles removed from students. However, we need great teachers who know research and policy, how to work with adults, how to listen, and how to lead in these positions.

What is the biggest challenge you are currently facing as a teacher? Spend some time thinking about this and then take a look at Figure 8.4.

- Are you struggling with how to reach particular students?
- Are you having difficulty working with colleagues or administrators?
- Do you feel like you are stagnant or overwhelmed?
- Do you feel like you are filling the classroom, motivating, demanding, and building important relationships?

If you are reading this with a group or a partner, spend time identifying a challenge for yourselves or your team. Ensure it is a big enough challenge that the time spent will be worthwhile individually or as a group. If you identify a group challenge, be sure to identify subchallenges for individual contribution. This needs to be a tangible challenge for everyone.

After the challenge has been identified, spend some time reflecting on barriers to overcoming the challenge.

- What about you might keep you from meeting the challenge?
- What about others around you might be an inhibiting factor?
- Are there resources that are lacking?

Be honest—particularly with the internal barriers you face. If you are not honest, you are unlikely to make real progress toward a solution.

Next, examine yourself, others, and resources to determine the assets you have at your disposal.

- What skills do you have that you personally bring to the challenge?
- What can others contribute?
- Who and what is in your personal learning network (PLN)?

This is an important step as this will help determine the likelihood of arriving at a workable solution. Again, honesty is crucial as overselling or underselling our assets can distort our map.

After identifying barriers and assets, determine what technical solutions could possibly be suggested. Maybe it would help to think like an administrator here.

- What would the principal tell you?
- How have these challenges been met before?
- What suggestions do research or others in your PLN suggest?

There may be a nugget of an idea here that could be expanded upon to include your school context. Unless you have an extremely straightforward challenge, it is unlikely that any one technical change would be enough to be considered a solution.

FIGURE 8.4 Expert Novice Map

Challenge	Barriers			Technical Solutions	Expert Novice Solutions
	Self	Others	Resources		
	Assets				
	Self	Others	Resources		

After listing all of the possible technical solutions, move to the expert novice solutions. In this column, you might build on several technical solutions, or you might describe an entirely innovative solution that will work for you and your students.

Figure 8.5 is a sample table that walks you through the challenge that someone in Andrew Berndt's position might have faced. Andrew was the math teacher who flipped his classroom. He did not complete this chart, but this is an example of how someone in his position might have completed it. The key to this example is that the ultimate solution has considered barriers, typical quick fixes, and then a more meaningful and comprehensive solution based on the teacher's expertise. Also, if your challenge is one that takes you beyond your classroom into new forms of leadership, your map is going to look different than Andrew's. In fact, every expert novice map will look different because it is dependent on the individual and his context.

Notice that the expert novice solution here is not to simply flip the classroom. Flipping the classroom alone may have no effect or even a negative effect. The solution here is to provide students more time to struggle, collaborate, and problem solve. The vehicle that creates this additional space is moving some of the "teacher talk" out of the class period through online tutorials.

Never Lose Your Novice Self

I hope you are already embracing your novice mindset, applying the Four Rs to practice, and that you will do this over an amazing career in education. Hopefully, there have been some practical takeaways from the reading, but the "Expert Novice Map" is indicative of the way I hope you will embrace the challenges you will face. As you implement your solution, be sure to find a group of colleagues from whom you can get feedback. You will need to make midcourse corrections. One great thing about the many difficulties in our education system is that we will never run out of future challenges and should never get bored as we move toward expertise. Figure 8.6 is a reminder of how this is supposed to work.

Even though I spend a bulk of my time as a college professor in a teacher preparation program, to keep myself grounded and relevant, every year I teach science in public school classrooms. I bring my preservice teachers whenever possible so that they get a chance to observe me teaching students

> One great thing about the many difficulties in our education system is that we will never run out of future challenges.

before they are observed by me. I love teaching science to elementary and middle school students because they get so excited and engaged. One year, I was teaching the inquiry-based unit to a combined group of fifty-five students in one classroom. This was challenging, but I was feeling particularly good about my teaching because of one student in particular. He was new to the

FIGURE 8.5 Expert Novice Map—Hypothetical Math Teacher Example

Challenge	Barriers			Technical Solutions	Expert Novice Solutions
	Self	Others	Resources		
My students are not learning and applying mathematical concepts at a sufficient level of depth.	• I am a new teacher, and I have a desire to be liked by my students. • I worked very hard last year on my lessons, and I will have to completely redesign them this year. • I have never learned in a flipped classroom.	• Everyone else in my department delivers math content the way I did last year. • My principal and colleagues think I did a good job my first year. • Students learned and they and their parents were happy.	• I am not sure what resources are available to me. • There is not extensive amount of collaboration in the math department. • I cannot buy new textbooks or materials. • I do not have a great deal of time.	• Change my assessments to measure a minimum level of understanding. • Provide more time after school and at lunch for students to come in for help. • Allow more time for students to work together. • Flip the classroom.	• As a teacher, I will talk less and allow more time for students to work through problems. • I will provide help and scaffold experiences that encourage exploration and struggle to make meaning. • I will create additional space for this collaboration by flipping my classroom and working example problems that can be viewed online.
	Assets				
	Self	Others	Resources		
	• I have a lot of energy and mathematical expertise. • I have some credibility after a successful first year. • I have an interest in the flipped classroom.	• My department chair and colleagues are supportive. • My students trust me. • There are other teachers in my PLN who have more effectively engaged their students.	• There are online resources and tools for animating problems and recording voiceovers. • My school just implemented a one-to-one technology initiative so every student has access to a computer.		

FIGURE 8.6   The Iterative Theory of Action

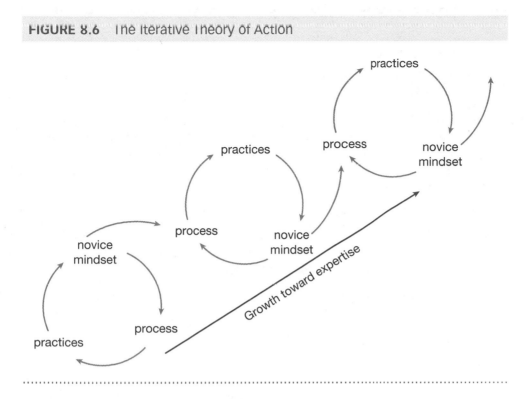

United States from East Asia. He did not speak any English. In fact, no adults in the district spoke his language. Throughout the unit, he seemed to be engaging in the labs and demonstrations, smiling, and working with his team. On one of the last days of the unit, we were discussing some key information when I looked back and saw him madly taking notes on his study guide.

Wow, science had broken through the language barrier, and it seemed he was completely engrossed in recording what I was saying and writing!

Teaching English learners is not that challenging, I thought to myself.

I walked to the back of the class to observe his note taking. However, he was not taking notes. He had created a detailed set of drawings of the Incredible Hulk that had nothing to do with physical science.

Although the student clearly was not on task, I am clearly making progress:

- I did not need a video to tell me he was not engaged.
- The classroom was not on fire.
- There wasn't vomit on anyone.

I hope you will embrace the challenges you will face with honesty, vulnerability, curiosity, hope, and a sense of humor. Our profession and our students need you.

Key Takeaways and Fearless Practices

- Don't think of this book as a collection of technical solutions—take advantage of your novice mindset.

- Technical solutions alone cannot solve adaptive challenges—the answer lies in changing our mindset and process related to teaching, learning, and ourselves. Get better in your own classroom by using assessment and what you know will work best for your students. You have to find your own way.

- Innovate. You know your students better than anyone. Determine what is best for them and move forward.

- Spread your expertise. As you grow, go public with what you have learned. Invite the feedback of others.

- Influence policy. Teachers need to influence, implement, and determine decisions related to the classroom.

- Never stop learning. One of the best ways to learn is to take on new challenges.

- Listen more than you speak. You are always a learner.

- Stretch yourself beyond what is comfortable by overcoming fear.

- Don't embrace every new change. Sometimes the wisest course of action is to take a principled stand.

- Find one challenge and start attacking it with the assets at your disposal.

- Keep a sense of humor.

Open-Ended Case Study

You are the open-ended case study at the end of this chapter. If you have not already completed your expert novice map, do that now. Most of the expert novice map consists of reflection. When you arrive at an expert novice solution, that is your chance to take a well-reasoned risk. What is next is up to you.

- Will you close this book without identifying your next solution and resign yourself to a year of stagnation?

I hope not because those years of stagnation can lead to unfulfilling careers.

Or,

- Will you continue down a path that leads to growth and change?

I hope you will choose growth because our students need us to be expert novices who lead boldly and encourage them to do the same.

Reflect

- What challenge have you identified?
- How will you engage your PLN as you implement your solution?
- Who can you specifically count on for support and feedback as you move forward?
- Where might your career lead you if you continue to grow as an expert novice?

Risk: 3-2-1 Action Steps

3:   Complete your expert novice map!

Possible steps:

- Complete your expert novice map!
- Determine if your solution is one that is in the classroom, in others' classrooms, or beyond the classroom.
- Based on your decision, identify at least one appropriate person who can hold you accountable to implement your expert novice solution.

2:   Reflect on your progress as you implement your solution.

Possible steps:

- Determine what is working and what is not.
- Identify if you or others are doing something that is undermining the success of your solution.

1:   Make midcourse corrections and start thinking of what your next challenge might be. Our education system is a panoply of challenges that ensure our work should always be meaningful and will never be boring.

Possible steps:

- Check in with your colleague(s) to get feedback on your progress and start thinking of challenges you can address together.

Revise or Reject

After taking a risk, determine what to do next. Was it worthy of revision or rejection?

☐ Reject   ☐ Revise

Write down a few notes about what worked, what did not, and what you might change.

A Guide to
The Novice Advantage
Fearless Practice for Every Teacher

Any good book I have ever read has caused me to do two things:

1. Think about the world differently.
2. Talk to others about what I am reading.

I hope *The Novice Advantage: Fearless Practice for Every Teacher* will do that for you. The book is written as a conversation between us as teachers. This should catalyze conversations with other teachers. The novice advantage is an expansive view of teaching that is always exciting when we grow together. In order to help facilitate that process, I have included many tools in the book including "fearless reflections" that require the reader to take a position, reflection questions, action steps, and open-ended case studies. In addition, I have developed this guide.

This guide is designed to use with other teachers whom you choose to walk with for a while on your professional journey—life is much better that way, and the book will be enriched by the experience of others. This will serve as a facilitator's guide for discussion and as a tool for reflection and action. Some possible discussion starters for each chapter are included. The 4Rs, reflect, risk, revise or reject, which are introduced in more detail in Chapter 3, provide the structure of the guide to help you arrive at key takeaways and actions.

Please email me at jonathan.m.eckert@gmail.com or go to jonathanmeckert.com for more resources, to ask questions, or to provide feedback.

Enjoy the conversation!
Jon Eckert

REFLECTING FEARLESSLY TOGETHER: DISCUSSION STARTERS

Preface:

1. Describe three "first days" you have had. How have those days changed you as a teacher?

2. What is the newest challenge that you have taken on as an opportunity to grow? How has that changed you?

Chapter 1: Cringeworthy Moments—Why Would I Want to Be a Novice?

1. What are the biggest challenges you face as a teacher?

2. What are the advantages of the novice mindset when facing these challenges?

3. Theodore Roosevelt talks about "avoiding the gray twilight." As a teacher, what is your "gray twilight" that should be avoided?

Chapter 2: Embrace the Novice Mindset

1. What is your novice mindset score out of 40 points? Using markers or stickers (dot down), visually represent where you fall on the mindset scale. What is the range of your team's scores?

2. How can you develop the novice mindset in yourself? Colleagues? Students?

Chapter 3: Reflect. Risk. Revise or Reject.

1. What is one idea that you have tried and rejected?

2. How does your personal learning network need to grow?

Chapter 4: Fill the Classroom

1. What is one way you have been successful in creating space for students? How could you create even more space? What concerns you about creating space for students?

2. When are students most engaged in your class? How could you increase the amount of time where students are highly engaged?

Chapter 5: Motivate Pragmatically

1. As a student, in which classes were you most motivated to learn? What did these classes have in common?

2. How have you handled choices and consequences in your classroom? What has worked? Why?

Chapter 6: Expect More

1. What percentage of teachers believes they have high expectations for students?

2. Think about the press and support 2x2. Where do you most need to grow—in your willingness to consistently demand more of students or in your ability to provide support?

3. How would only accepting students' best work, not giving zeros, and requiring everyone to answer affect your teaching?

Chapter 7: Build Important Relationships

1. How can you find and celebrate what is fascinating about your students?

2. What members of your school community do you need to build relationships with? How will you go about doing this?

Chapter 8: Become an Expert Novice

1. Who can you specifically count on for support and feedback as you move forward?

2. Where might your career lead you if you continue to grow as an expert novice?

Reflect	*What key takeaways, quotes, or questions did you find? Were there any surprises or insights from the Fearless Reflection boxes? Be sure to write down page numbers to share.*	
Risk	*What have you done or will you do to take a risk? This might be saying "yes" to something new, or "no" to something popular. Who can you enlist to take the risk with you or give you feedback?*	
Revise or Reject	*What ideas from the chapter or from your practice do you need to develop further? Are there any ideas that should be rejected? Who can you enlist for help and feedback?*	
Fearless Action	*After discussion, individually or as a team, what concrete step(s) will you take in your classroom to grow? Commit to a timeline for action with formative checks.*	

Created by Jon Eckert 2015

Reflect	*What key takeaways, quotes, or questions did you find? Were there any surprises or insights from the Fearless Reflection boxes? Be sure to write down page numbers to share.*	
Risk	*What have you done or will you do to take a risk? This might be saying "yes" to something new, or "no" to something popular. Who can you enlist to take the risk with you or give you feedback?*	
Revise or Reject	*What ideas from the chapter or from your practice do you need to develop further? Are there any ideas that should be rejected? Who can you enlist for help and feedback?*	
Fearless Action	*After discussion, individually or as a team, what concrete step(s) will you take in your classroom to grow? Commit to a timeline for action with formative checks.*	

Created by Jon Eckert 2015

Reflect	*What key takeaways, quotes, or questions did you find? Were there any surprises or insights from the Fearless Reflection boxes? Be sure to write down page numbers to share.*	
Risk	*What have you done or will you do to take a risk? This might be saying "yes" to something new, or "no" to something popular. Who can you enlist to take the risk with you or give you feedback?*	
Revise or Reject	*What ideas from the chapter or from your practice do you need to develop further? Are there any ideas that should be rejected? Who can you enlist for help and feedback?*	
Fearless Action	*After discussion, individually or as a team, what concrete step(s) will you take in your classroom to grow? Commit to a timeline for action with formative checks.*	

Created by Jon Eckert 2015

Reflect	*What key takeaways, quotes, or questions did you find? Were there any surprises or insights from the Fearless Reflection boxes? Be sure to write down page numbers to share.*	
Risk	*What have you done or will you do to take a risk? This might be saying "yes" to something new, or "no" to something popular. Who can you enlist to take the risk with you or give you feedback?*	
Revise or Reject	*What ideas from the chapter or from your practice do you need to develop further? Are there any ideas that should be rejected? Who can you enlist for help and feedback?*	
Fearless Action	*After discussion, individually or as a team, what concrete step(s) will you take in your classroom to grow? Commit to a timeline for action with formative checks.*	

Created by Jon Eckert 2015

Reflect	*What key takeaways, quotes, or questions did you find? Were there any surprises or insights from the Fearless Reflection boxes? Be sure to write down page numbers to share.*	
Risk	*What have you done or will you do to take a risk? This might be saying "yes" to something new, or "no" to something popular. Who can you enlist to take the risk with you or give you feedback?*	
Revise or Reject	*What ideas from the chapter or from your practice do you need to develop further? Are there any ideas that should be rejected? Who can you enlist for help and feedback?*	
Fearless Action	*After discussion, individually or as a team, what concrete step(s) will you take in your classroom to grow? Commit to a timeline for action with formative checks.*	

Created by Jon Eckert 2015

Reflect	*What key takeaways, quotes, or questions did you find? Were there any surprises or insights from the Fearless Reflection boxes? Be sure to write down page numbers to share.*	
Risk	*What have you done or will you do to take a risk? This might be saying "yes" to something new, or "no" to something popular. Who can you enlist to take the risk with you or give you feedback?*	
Revise or Reject	*What ideas from the chapter or from your practice do you need to develop further? Are there any ideas that should be rejected? Who can you enlist for help and feedback?*	
Fearless Action	*After discussion, individually or as a team, what concrete step(s) will you take in your classroom to grow? Commit to a timeline for action with formative checks.*	

Created by Jon Eckert 2015

Reflect	*What key takeaways, quotes, or questions did you find? Were there any surprises or insights from the Fearless Reflection boxes? Be sure to write down page numbers to share.*	
Risk	*What have you done or will you do to take a risk? This might be saying "yes" to something new, or "no" to something popular. Who can you enlist to take the risk with you or give you feedback?*	
Revise or Reject	*What ideas from the chapter or from your practice do you need to develop further? Are there any ideas that should be rejected? Who can you enlist for help and feedback?*	
Fearless Action	*After discussion, individually or as a team, what concrete step(s) will you take in your classroom to grow? Commit to a timeline for action with formative checks.*	

Created by Jon Eckert 2015

CHAPTER 8: Become an Expert Novice

After reading the chapter, complete the Expert Novice Map below to address the most pressing challenge you are facing. This can be done individually or as a team, but you need to identify someone to give you feedback about your map and your subsequent progress.

Challenge	Barriers			Technical Solutions	Expert Novice Solutions
	Self	Others	Resources		
	Assets				
	Self	Others	Resources		

References

Alexandrou, A., & Swaffield, S. (2014). *Teacher leadership and professional development*. New York, NY: Routledge.

American Statistical Association. (2014). ASA statement on using value-added models on educational assessment. American Statistical Association. Retrieved from http://vamboozled.com/wp-content/uploads/2014/03/ASA_VAM_Statement.pdf

Andrea, C. D'. (2013). Limits on collective bargaining. *Education Next, 13*(4). Retrieved from http://educationnext.org/limits-on-collective-bargaining/

Arkansas Department of Education. (2014). *Jones Elementary School report card 2015*. Retrieved from http://adesrc.arkansas.gov/ReportCard/View?lea=7207041&schoolYear=2014

Ball, D. L., & Forzani, F. M. (2011). Building a common core for learning to teach, and connecting professional learning to practice. *American Educator, 68*(4), 17–21, 38–39.

Behrstock-Sherratt, E., Bassett, K., Olson, D., & Jacques, C. (2014). *From good to great: Exemplary teachers share perspectives on increasing teacher effectiveness across the career continuum*. Washington, DC: AIR. Retrieved from http://www.gtlcenter.org/sites/default/files/Good_to_Great_Report.pdf

Berliner, D. (2004). Expert teachers: Their characteristics, development and accomplishments. In R. Batllori i Obiols, A. E. Gomez Martinez, M. Oller i Freixa, & J. Pages i. Blanch (Eds.), *De la teoria. . . . a l'aula: Formacio del professorat ensenyament de las ciències socials* (pp. 13–28). Barcelona, Spain: Departament de Didàctica de la Llengua de la Literatura I de les Ciències Socials, Universitat Autònoma de Barcelona.

Berry, B. (2010). *Teaching 2030: What we must do for our students and public schools*. New York, NY: Teachers College Press.

Berry, B., Byrd, A., & Wieder, A. (2013). *Teacherpreneurs: Innovative teachers who lead but don't leave*. San Francisco, CA: Jossey-Bass.

Berry, B., & Eckert, J. (2012). Creating teacher incentives for school excellence and equity. *Boulder, CO: National Education Policy Center*. Retrieved from http://nepc.colorado.edu/publication/creating-teacher-incentives

Black, P., Harrison, C., Marshall, B., & William, D. (2004). Working inside the black box: Assessment for learning in the classroom. *Phi Delta Kappan, 86*(1), 9–21.

Bondy, E., & Ross, D. D. (2008). The teacher as warm demander. *Educational Leadership, 66*(1), 54–58.

Bondy, E., Ross, D. D., Hambacher, E., & Acosta, M. (2012). Becoming warm demanders: Perspectives and practices of first year teachers. *Urban Education, 48*(3), 420–450. http://doi.org/10.1177/0042085912456846

Brown, P. C., Roediger, H. L., & McDaniel, M. A. (2014). *Make it stick: The science of successful learning*. Cambridge, MA: Belknap Press.

Bryk, A., & Schneider, B. (2002). *Trust in schools: A core resource for improvement.* New York, NY: Russell Sage.

Chappuis, J., Stiggins, R. J., Chappuis, S., & Arter, J. A. (2006). *Classroom assessment for student learning: Doing it right—using it well.* Portland, OR: Educational Testing Services.

Costrell, R. M., & Podgursky, M. (2009). Teacher retirement benefits. *Education Next*, 9(2). Retrieved from http://educationnext.org/teacher-retirement-benefits/

Crowther, F., Ferguson, M., & Hann, L. (2009). *Developing teacher leaders: How teacher leadership enhances school success.* Thousand Oaks, CA: Corwin.

Deci, E., & Flaste, R. (1995). *Why we do what we do: Understanding self-motivation.* New York, NY: Penguin Group.

Duckworth, A. L., Peterson, C., Matthews, M. D., & Kelly, D. R. (2007). Grit: Perseverance and passion for long-term goals. *Journal of Personality and Social Psychology*, 92(6), 1087–1101.

Duke, D. (2008). How do you turn around a low-performing school? Presented at the ASCD Annual Conference, New Orleans, LA.

Dweck, C. S. (2006). *Mindset: The new psychology of success.* New York, NY: Ballantine Books.

Eckert, J. (2010). Performance-based compensation: Design and implementation at six teacher incentive fund sites. Bill & Melinda Gates Foundation. Retrieved from http://www.niet.org/assets/Publications/performance-based-compensation-tif.pdf?processed=1

Eckert, J. (2013). Increasing educator effectiveness: Lessons learned from selected TIF sites. National Institute for Excellence in Teaching. Retrieved from http://www.niet.org/assets/Publications/increasing-educator-effectiveness-lessons-learned-from-teacher-incentive-fund-sites.pdf?processed=1

Eckert, J. (2016). Student growth measures: A view from the classroom. In K. Kappler-Hewitt & A. Amrein-Beardsley (Eds.), *Student growth measures in policy and practice.*

Eckert, J., & Dabrowski, J. (2010). Should value-added measures be used for performance pay? *Phi Delta Kappan*, 91(8), 88–92.

Eckert, J., & Smylie, M. A. (2014). Conditions for leadership in learning organizations. Presented at the University Council on Educational Administration Annual Conference, Washington, DC.

Education Week Research Center. (2014). *Engaging students for success: Findings from a national survey.* Bethesda, MD: Editorial Projects in Education Inc. Retrieved from http://www.edweek.org/media/ewrc_engagingstudents_2014.pdf

Ericsson, K. A., Krampe, R. T., & Tesch-Romer, C. (1993). The role of deliberate practice in the acquisition of expert performance. *Psychological Review*, 100(3), 363–406.

Esquith, R. (2003). *There are no shortcuts.* New York, NY: Anchor Books.

Esquith, R. (2007). *Teach like your hair's on fire: The methods and madness inside room 56.* New York, NY: Viking.

Ferguson, R. F., & Danielson, C. (2014). How framework for teaching and tripod 7Cs evidence distinguish key components of effective teaching. In T. J. Kane, K. A. Kerr, & R. C. Pianta (Eds.), *Designing teacher evaluation systems: New guidance from the Measures of Effective Teaching Project* (pp. 98–143). San Francisco, CA: Jossey-Bass.

Gall, M. D. (1984). Synthesis of research on teachers' questioning. *Educational Leadership*, 42(3), 40–47.

Gawande, A. (2007). *Better: A surgeon's notes on performance*. Metropolitan Books.

Gladwell, M. (2008). *Outliers: The story of success*. New York, NY: Bay Back Books.

Goldstein, D. (2014). *The teacher wars: A history of America's most embattled profession*. New York, NY: Doubleday.

Graesser, A. C., & Person, N. K. (1994). Question asking during tutoring. *American Educational Research Journal, 31*(1), 104–137.

Guthrie, J. T. (2008). *Engaging adolescents in reading*. Thousand Oaks, CA: Corwin.

Hargreaves, A., & Fullan, M. (2012). *Professional capital: Transforming teaching in every school*. New York, NY: Teachers College Press.

Hatch, T., Ahmed, D., Lieberman, A., Faigenbaum, D., White, M. E., & Pointer Mace, D. H. (Eds.). (2005). *Going public with our teaching: An anthology of practice*. New York, NY: Teachers College Press.

Hattie, J. (2012). *Visible learning for teachers: Maximizing impact on learning*. London, England: Routledge.

Hattie, J., & Yates, G. (2014). *Visible learning and the science of how we learn*. New York, NY: Routledge.

Ho, A. D., Reich, J., Nesterko, S., Seaton, D. T., Mullaney, T., Waldo, J., & Chuang, I. (2014). *HarvardX and MITx: The first year of open online courses*. HarvardX and MITx Working Paper No. 1. Retrieved from http://dx.doi.org/10.2139/ssrn.2381263

Ingersoll, R., Merrill, L., & Stuckey, D. (2014). *Seven trends: The transformation of the teaching force, updated April 2014. CPRE Report* (No. (#RR-80)). Philadelphia: Consortium for Policy Research in Education, University of Pennsylvania. Retrieved from http://www.cpre.org/sites/default/files/workingpapers/1506_7trendsapril2014.pdf

Jackson, R. R. (2009). *Never work harder than your students: And other principles of great teaching*. Alexandria, VA: Association for Supervision and Curriculum Development.

Jensen, B., Hunter, J., Sonnemann, J., & Cooper, S. (2014). *Making time for great teaching*. Melbourne, Australia: Grattan Institute.

Kahneman, D. (2011). *Thinking, fast and slow*. New York, NY: Farrar, Straus and Giroux.

Kane, T. J., Kerr, K. A., & Pianta, R. C. (2014). *Designing teacher evaluation systems: New guidance from the Measures of Effective Teaching Project*. San Francisco, CA: Jossey-Bass.

Karpicke, J. D. (2012). Retrieval-based learning: Active retrieval promotes meaningful learning. *Current Directions in Psychological Science, 21*(3), 157–163.

Kegan, R., & Lahey, L. L. (2009). *Immunity to change: How to overcome it and unlock the potential in yourself and your organization*. Boston, MA: Harvard Business Press.

Knight, J. (2014). *Focus on teaching: Using video for high-impact teaching*. Thousand Oaks, CA: Corwin.

Kohn, A. (1994). The risk of rewards. *ERIC Digest*. Retrieved from http://www.alfiekohn.org/teaching/ror.htm

Kounin, J. S. (1970). *Discipline and group management in classrooms*. Huntington, NY: R.E. Krieger.

Krueger, A., & Sutton, J. (Eds.). (2001). *EDThoughts: What we know about science teaching and learning*. Aurora, CO: Mid-continent Research for Education and Learning.

Ladd, H. F., & Sorensen, L. C. (2014). Returns to teacher experience: Student achievement and motivation in middle school. CALDER Working Paper No. 112. Retrieved from http://www.caldercenter.org/sites/default/files/WP-112_final.pdf

Lemov, D. (2010). *Teach like a champion: 49 techniques that put students on the path to college.* San Francisco, CA: Jossey-Bass.

Lemov, D. (2015). *Teach like a champion 2.0: 62 techniques that put students on the path to college.* San Francisco, CA: Jossey-Bass.

Lieberman, A., & Miller, L. (2004). *Teacher leadership.* San Francisco, CA: Jossey-Bass.

Lortie, D. (1975). *Schoolteacher: A sociological inquiry.* New York, NY: John Wiley.

Martin, Jr, R. E., Wood, G. H., & Stevens, E. W. (1988). *An introduction to teaching: A question of commitment.* Needham Heights, MA: Allyn and Bacon.

Marzano, R. J., Pickering, D. J., & Heflebower, T. (2011). *The highly engaged classroom.* Bloomington, IN: Marzano Research Library.

Matthews, J. (1988). *Escalante: The best teacher in America.* New York, NY: Henry Holt.

MetLife, (2012). The MetLife survey of the American teacher: Teachers, parents and the Economy. Retrieved from https://www.metlife.com/assets/cao/contributions/foundation/american-teacher/MetLife-Teacher-Survey-2011.pdf

MetLife. (2013). The MetLife Survey of the American teacher: Challenges for School Leadership. MetLife. Retrieved from https://www.metlife.com/assets/cao/foundation/MetLife-Teacher-Survey-2012.pdf

Moeny, J. (2015). Award-winning educator decries current teaching climate. *Education Week, 34*(26), 8.

Moss, C., & Burhart, S. (2012). *Learning Targets: Helping students aim for understanding in today's lesson.* Alexandria, VA: Association for Supervision and Curriculum Development.

Murphy, J. (2005). *Connecting teacher leadership and school improvement.* Thousand Oaks, CA: Corwin.

National Research Council. (2000). *How people learn: Brain, mind, experience, and school (Expanded Ed.).* Washington, DC: National Academies Press.

Palmer, P. (1993). *To know as we are known: Education as a spiritual journey.* San Francisco, CA: Jossey-Bass.

Palmer, P. (2007). *The courage to teach.* San Francisco, CA: Jossey-Bass.

Palmer, P. (2015). Begin again: On getting unstuck. Retrieved from http://www.onbeing.org/blog/parker-palmer-begin-again-on-getting-unstuck/8210).

Papay, J. P., & Kraft, M. A. (in press). Productivity returns to experience in the teacher labor market: Methodological challenges and new evidence on long-term career improvement. *Journal of Public Economics.*

Pennington, K. (2013). *The landscape of today's teachers shaping policy.* Washington, DC: The Center for American Progress.

Pianta, R. C., & Stuhlman, M. W. (2004). Teacher-child relationships and children's success in the first years of school. *School Psychology Review, 33*(3), 444–458.

Pierson, Rita. (2013, May). Every kid needs a champion. *TED.* Retrieved from https://www.ted.com/talks/rita_pierson_every_kid_needs_a_champion?language=en

Pink, D. (2009). *Drive: The surprising truth about what motivates us.* New York, NY: Riverhead Books.

Popham, W. J. (2008). *Transformative assessment.* Alexandria, VA: Association for Supervision and Curriculum Development.

Quaglia, R. J., & Corso, M. J. (2014). *Student voice: The instrument of change.* Thousand Oaks, CA: Corwin.

Reeves, D. (2011). *Elements of grading: A guide to effective practice.* Bloomington, IL: Solution Tree Press.

Reynolds, B. (1998). *The letters of Dorothy Sayers: Volume three 1944–1950.* London, England: Hodder & Stoughton.

Richards, E. (2015, May 27). Provision slipped into budget dilutes teacher license rules. *Milwaukee Journal Sentinel.* Milwaukee, WI. Retrieved from http://www.jsonline.com/news/education/late-night-budget-action-dillutes-teacher-license-rules-b99508103z1-305176951.html

Riddell, K. (2014, September 1). Generous teacher pensions continue as financial crisis worsens. *The Washington Times.* Retrieved from http://www.washington-times.com/news/2014/sep/1/generous-teacher-pensions-continue-as-illinois-fin/?page=all

Riley, J. P. (1986). The effects of teachers' wait-time and knowledge comprehension questioning on science achievement. *Journal of Research in Science Teaching, 23*(4), 335–342.

Rodriguez, V., & Fitzpatrick, M. (2014). *The teaching brain: An evolutionary trait at the heart of teaching.* New York, NY: The New Press.

Ronfeldt, M., Farmer, S. O., McQueen, K., & Grissom, J. A. (2015). Teacher collaboration in instructional teams and student achievement. *American Educational Research Journal, 52*(3), 475–514.

Rowe, M. B. (1986). Wait time: Slowing down may be a way of speeding up! *Journal of Teacher Education, 37*(1), 43–50.

Sanders, W. L., & Horn, S. P. (1994). The Tennessee value-added assessment system (TVAAS): Mixed-model methodology in educational assessment. *Journal of Personnel Evaluation in Education, 8,* 299–311.

Shulman, L. (1986). Those who understand: Knowledge growth in teaching. *Educational Research, 15*(2), 4–14.

Silver, D., Berchemeyer, J. C., & Baenen, J. R. (2014). *Deliberate optimism: Reclaiming the joy in education.* Thousand Oaks, CA: Corwin.

Smith, R., & Lambert, M. (2008). Assuming the best. *Educational Leadership, 66*(1), 16–21.

Smylie, M. (2010). *Continuous school improvement.* Thousand Oaks, CA: Corwin.

Spiegel, A. (2012). *Struggle for smarts? How Eastern and Western cultures tackle learning.* Retrieved from http://www.npr.org/blogs/health/2012/11/12/164793058/struggle-for-smarts-how-eastern-and-western-cultures-tackle-learning

Stewart, J. (2015, June 18). A fearless culture fuels U.S. tech giants. *New York Times,* p. B1.

Surowiecki, J. (2014, November 10). Better all the time: How the "performance revolution" came to athletics-and beyond. *The New Yorker.* Retrieved from http://www.newyorker.com/magazine/2014/11/10/better-time

Tatum, A. W. (2006). Engaging African American males in reading. *Educational Leadership, 63*(5), 44–49.

The New Teacher Project. (2015). *The mirage: Confronting the hard truth about our quest for teacher development.* The New Teacher Project. Retrieved from http://tntp.org/assets/documents/TNTP-Mirage_2015.pdf

Tomlinson, C., & Moon, T. (2013). *Assessment and student success in a differentiated classroom.* Alexandria, VA: Association for Supervision and Curriculum Development.

Tough, P. (2012). *How children succeed: Grit, curiosity, and the hidden power of character*. New York, NY: Mariner.

U.S. Department of Education (n.d.). Teaching ambassador fellowship. Retrieved from http://www2.ed.gov/programs/teacherfellowship/fellows/houtchens.html

U.S. Department of Education, National Center for Education Statistics. (2015). *The condition of education 2015* (No. (NCES 2015-144)). Washington, DC: U.S. Department of Education. Retrieved from https://nces.ed.gov/fastfacts/display .asp?id=77

Wiggins, G. (2012). Seven keys to effective feedback. *Educational Leadership*, 70(1), 10–16.

Wiggins, G., & McTighe, J. (1998). *Understanding by Design*. Alexandria, VA: Association for Supervision and Curriculum Development.

Wiggins, G., & McTighe, J. (2005). *Understanding by Design*. Alexandria, VA: Association for Supervision and Curriculum Development.

Willingham, D. T. (2009). *Why don't students like school?* San Francisco, CA: Jossey-Bass.

Wilson, B. L., & Corbett, H. D. (2001). *Listening to urban kids: School reform and the teachers they want*. Albany: State University of New York Press.

Wiseman, L. (2014). *Rookie smarts: Why learning beats knowing in the new game of work*. New York, NY: Harper Business.

Wong, H. K., & Wong, R. T. (2009). *The first days of school*. Mountain View, CA: Harry K. Wong Publications.

Woo, E. (2010, March 31). Jaime Escalante dies at 79; math teacher who challenged East L.A. students to "Stand and Deliver." *Los Angeles Times*, p. W.

York-Barr, J., & Duke, D. (2004). What do we know about teacher leadership? Findings from two decades of scholarship. *Review of Educational Research*, 74(3), 255–316.

Index

A SAGE Publishing Company

CORWIN HAS ONE MISSION: to enhance education through intentional professional learning.

We build long-term relationships with our authors, educators, clients, and associations who partner with us to develop and continuously improve the best evidence-based practices that establish and support lifelong learning.